Contents

POLITICS
OF THE IRISH
CONSTITUTION

BASIL CHUBB

Institute of Public Administration

Published by
Institute of Public Administration
57-61 Lansdowne Road
Dublin 4

ISBN 1-872002-85-4

Cover design by Butler Claffey Design

A CIP catalogue record for this
book is available from the
British Library.

Origination by Computertype Limited, Dublin
Printed by Leinster Leader, Naas,
Co. Kildare, Republic of Ireland

Acknowledgements

In parts of this book I have made much use of the work of colleagues; in particular John Bowman (in chapter 3), John Whyte (in chapters 4 and 5), Gerard Hogan (in chapters 6 and 8), and John Temple Lang of the Commission of the European Communities, DGIV (in chapter 8). I am particularly indebted to Gerard Hogan and other colleagues in the School of Law in Trinity College who have answered my many questions. Brian Farrell read the manuscript and offered comments and I am grateful to him. I thank Miriam Nestor who has worked with me during the preparation of the book.

— 1 —

Constitutions as a Political Force

FOR THE PEOPLE of Ireland, as for those of most countries, 'the constitution' is 'a selection of the legal rules which govern the government of that country and which have been embodied in a document.'[1] *Bunreacht na hEireann (Constitution of Ireland)*, enacted in 1937, is such a document. As is the case also in most countries, though not all, the Constitution of Ireland has a higher legal status than other laws. In Ireland's case there is an important exception to this. In common with the countries of the European Communities, Community law takes precedence over the laws of the member states. Again, in most countries — and Ireland is one of these — such documents are regarded as being both 'the fundamental law of the land' and 'a kind of higher law.'[2] The Constitution of Ireland cannot be altered or repealed in the manner of ordinary legislation, for besides the approval of both houses of the Oireachtas, such changes require the consent of a majority of the electors at a referendum.

It is necessary to notice, however, that this definition refers to a selection of the rules that govern the government. Unlike most ordinary people, lawyers and political scientists do not confine their use of the word constitution to an identifiable document. For them:

> the terms 'constitution' and 'constitutional law' can be and often are used in a wider sense, to describe matters which are thought to be of 'constitutional' importance — importance that is to say, in understanding what lies behind and beyond the 'constitution', so that the constitution can be understood as a central feature, but not the sole feature, of the rules regulating the system of government.[3]

1

The form in which such matters are expressed might be statute laws or other legal instruments, rulings of the courts in 'constitutional' cases, European Community law, or even statements of practice or norms that are not formal rules at all. Items in this last category are often called 'conventions' which might be defined as practices or norms that, though they are not enforced by the courts, are accepted as the proper way to behave and are effective in controlling the operation of government.

Thus we have a second meaning of the word constitution. It is 'the system of laws, customs and conventions which define the composition and powers of organs of the state and regulate the relations of the various state organs with one another and with the private citizen.'[4] Clearly this definition subsumes the written document, but that document is likely to include the key elements of the system and to be its foundation. Some writers go further and say that the document 'can more appropriately be considered as a form in which the constitution is expressed rather than as a definition of the term itself.'[5] There is good reason for British writers at least to argue thus because the United Kingdom, unlike most countries, does not have the basic principles and rules of its system codified in a single document and in that country it is only in the wider sense that the word constitution can be used.

The view that a document or charter such as *Bunreacht na hEireann (Constitution of Ireland)* is best thought of as only a form — albeit the major form — in which the constitution is expressed might have wider merit however. Obviously, any selection of rules embodied in a document like this cannot be operated in isolation, but is a part — the key part — of the whole system of government and such a system must inevitably be both organic and dynamic. Unless a country is ruled by an alien power with no regard for the values or wishes of the indigenous people or by an autocratic, conservative minority regime, its political system and its laws will tend to reflect, perhaps with some delays, the changing standards and beliefs of the people, or at least of the politically dominant group. It will necessarily, therefore, have to adapt to changing social conditions and political exigencies.

In any case, the statements in a basic constitutional document are often couched in general even abstract terms and there is a need to have them applied authoritatively to particular circumstances as they arise. Thus there builds up around such a document a penumbra of constitutional law in the form of statutes, statutory or other legal instruments, or case-by-case decisions by the courts. This process of developing the basic constitutional laws enables the system to keep in tune with contemporary life and values and, consequently, to remain viable and legitimate. Carl Friedrich was right when he observed that 'too few people realize that every constitution is continually changing, even without formal amendment....'[6]

There is merit, then, in seeing the Irish constitution as more than merely the contents of a document entitled *Bunreacht na hEireann (Constitution of Ireland)*. Much less is it what you and I, reading it, think we have found there, for others with the legal right to do so — parliamentarians or judges — might have gone before us or, if we make an issue of it, might come after, to say with authority what is constitutional. A body of constitutional law and practice has been growing inexorably since 29 December 1937, the day on which Bunreacht na hEireann came into operation. Consequently, to take an example, if one wishes to explore the system of election to Dáil Eireann, it is necessary not only to consult Bunreacht ha hEireann (Article 16) but also the Electoral Acts (principally those of 1923 and 1963), at least one important judicial decision (O'Donovan v. Attorney General [1961] IR 114), and so on.

Although the terms 'constitutional' and 'constitutional law' seem not to be precise, it is possible to state at least in general terms what kinds of matters they might cover. A standard British work on constitutional law by de Smith lists the following: 'The location, conferment, distribution, exercise and limitation of authority and power among the organs of a state... matters of procedure as well as substance... guarantees of the rights and freedoms of individuals... ideological pronouncements — principles by which the state ought to be guided or to which it ought to aspire, and statements of the citizens' duties'.[7]

In Ireland's case we have *Bunreacht na hEireann* to refer to. It deals with the constitution, powers and procedures of the main organs of state such as the Oireachtas, the Government, the President, the Council of State and the courts, and it lays down rules about their relationship one with another; it includes the most important rules about voting, elections, referenda and the amendment of the Bunreacht itself; it creates official posts like that of the Comptroller and Auditor General (who audits and reports on the accounts of public authorities on behalf of the Oireachtas) and the Attorney General (who is the Government's adviser on matters of law and represents the state in important legal proceedings); it contains statements (mostly in Articles 40–44) of the fundamental rights of the citizens; it enunciates certain 'Directive Principles of Social Policy' (in Article 45) and there and elsewhere there are to be found some of those 'ideological pronouncements' mentioned by de Smith. In addition, there are also clauses about matters which might not be found in constitutions elsewhere but which seemed to the authors of *Bunreacht na hEireann* to be so important in the circumstances of Ireland at that time as to warrant inclusion. Not surprising to anyone who knows anything about Ireland at that time, these include declaratory articles about sovereignty, the extent of the national territory, the extent of application of the laws of the state 'pending the reintegration of the national territory', the name of the state, the status of the two languages used in the country, citizenship, and the colour of the national flag.

Because there are on many of these matters other rules of law, court judgements etc., a very large volume would be needed to mention and discuss them all. In fact such books exist: Most of them run to many hundreds of pages. Even a 'concise description' and 'easy explanation' , Brian Doolan's *Constitutional Law and Constitutional Rights in Ireland,* 2nd ed, (Dublin, 1988) contains over 300 pages.

II

Constitutions as we have defined them are a phenomenon of the modern world. It was not until the seventeenth century that the word evoked the idea of a document enunciating the fundamental framework of government and the basic principles by which a country should be governed. They were a direct product of liberalism and the revolt against the concentration of absolute and arbitrary political power that was such a feature of the development of the modern i.e. post-medieval, state. Constitutions became effective political devices when the politically dominant class in some of the rapidly developing countries of Western Europe and North America felt the need to define and delimit government; to accord a special status to particular rules of law regarded as fundamental; to insist that their governments, hitherto absolute rulers, should abide by the law; and to be willing themselves to do likewise.

The term 'constitutionalism' has come to signify this bundle of attitudes towards political power. It can be defined as 'an institutionalized system of effective, regularized restraints on governmental action.'[8] Where constitutionalism took root, the concept of the 'rule of law', the principle of 'the separation of powers' and the device of federalism together with declarations and charters of rights and liberties began to be canvassed and, where possible, defined and put into practice. In order to make these conditions effective they needed to be precisely formulated and hence the desire to have them in written form, to have them enacted into law and to have such laws given a special status. Where this political tradition became established constitutions are 'regulatory devices of great significance [and] ... do mold political behaviour. Most politics most of the time is conducted in accordance with such constitutional provisions.'[9]

The political attitudes that make up constitutionalism were encapsulated in *The Federalist Papers* of Alexander Hamilton, James Madison and John Jay, those formidable salvos in the war of words leading to the ratification of the Constitution of the United States of America in 1787-88. They are epitomized in the words of Madison in Paper no. 51:

> In framing a government which is to be administered by men over men, the great difficulty lies in this: you must first enable the government to control the governed; and in the next place oblige it to control itself. A dependence on the people is, no doubt, the primary control on the government; but experience has taught mankind the necessity of auxiliary precautions.[10]

Madison's reference to 'the people' in this passage points to a second feature of constitutionalism. It requires not only that power be delimited but also a recognition that the people ought to be sovereign. Popular sovereignty, together with liberalism were the burgeoning political doctrines of the west from the eighteenth century onward. Constitutionalism combines a recognition of the value of a constitution in limiting government by defining its power and prescribing its standards with the demand that this definition and these standards should be 'the formally enacted expression of the will of the people.... Modern constitutionalism, with the emerging liberalism whose ideology it shares, predicates naturally free, apolitical, and rights-bearing individuals who need and therefore establish governments that they can, may, and should control.'[11]

Constitutionalism is thus a feature of liberal-democratic communities but that is not to say that constitutions in the sense of written charters of basic law are not to be found in authoritarian countries. On the contrary: but there one finds what Karl Loewenstein called 'nominal' or 'semantic' constitutions as opposed to the 'normative' constitutions which are a feature of properly functioning liberal-democratic states.[12] In these countries a constitution once accepted is not only legal but is respected and obeyed and is therefore effective. It has a *normative* character and is in itself an important political force as a point of reference for government and governed alike:

> A normative constitution is not only valid in a legal sense, but it must be faithfully observed by all and have integrated itself into the state society: ... its norms govern the political process; or the power process adjusts itself to the norms... the constitution is like a suit that fits and that is actually worn.[13]

In practice in any country at any time the constitution will have this valuable normative character to the extent to which it embodies and reflects the traditions, culture and standards of the people of that country. Furthermore, a constitution might appropriately be judged by this criterion and by the extent to which it gives a comparatively clear and accurate account of the governmental system as it actually operates, together with a fair idea of the aims which governments do in fact pursue and of the limits within which they are in practice confined.

III

What is being suggested here is that the constitution of a liberal-democratic country like Ireland ought to have and maintain a normative character. To that end, it should first be at all times a congruent constitution, reflecting the basic beliefs, traditions and values of at least a large part of the population while not seriously affronting any minority; and, consequently, second, it must be capable of being adjusted to reflect major changes in community values and to adapt to important political changes, whether domestic or international. Constitutions need to be in process of continual development and at least periodic change. Constitutional development and modification, however effected, are therefore highly political matters and the proper concern of politics and politicians.

When it was enacted Bunreacht na hEireann mirrored quite well the traditions, culture and aspirations of the great majority of the people of the twenty-six counties which had constituted the Irish Free State: to a considerable extent it still does. As enacted, it reflected the formative influences upon Irish society. These were:

— the great legacy of the British connection that both geography and history made inevitable;

— nationalism, for it was enacted only sixteen years after the treaty that gave the twenty-six counties their independence and bequeathed Ireland as a whole its major problem;

— the Roman Catholic social teaching of the inter-war years which the Catholic population (then ninety-three per cent of the total) were conditioned to accept without question.

Because it was a congruent constitution in the context of the twenty-six county society of the thirties, it achieved a normative status and has been a political force for order and stability. That very congruence meant that it was not suitable for a state comprising the whole of Ireland for, as is now recognized (but was not then), there are two traditions in Ireland to be accommodated. It thus constituted a barrier to whatever chance of unity there might have been. Today, more than half a century on, many recognize this and look for appropriate changes.

Likewise, although the document of 1937 has been developed, first, by judicial interpretation that was initially hesitant but later more self-confident and assured and, second, more reluctantly and sporadically, by amendment, the fit of the Constitution even for the people of the Republic itself has become less good with the passage of time. In particular, the rapid industrialisation and urbanisation of the burgeoning sixties and early seventies transformed the country and began an inexorable process of cultural change. Accession to the European Communities in 1972 made the Republic subject to a new law to which domestic Irish law including the Constitution itself must defer. For all these reasons changes are increasingly canvassed and some of the proposed amendments raise obviously highly contentious political issues.

The making, development, amendment and even possible repeal and replacement of *Bunreacht na hEireann* were and are all highly political matters. That is the justification for this book. Its aim is to direct attention to the formative political influences that shaped the constitution in the mid-thirties; to identify the political forces that induced the comparatively modest changes that have been made and those that have inhibited change; to discuss the problem of how changes ought to be made; and to raise the political issues involved in making the more contentious changes that are perhaps now needed if the Constitution is to continue to be, in Edward McWhinney's words, 'law in action' and not just 'law in the book'.[14]

——— 2 ———

The British Connection and the Constitution

THE HISTORY OF Ireland has been dominated by one circumstance above all others, namely that it is an off-shore island of Great Britain. Geographically, it is a small island contiguous to a much larger one; historically, until recently, it was an integral part of the economic, cultural and political periphery of the United Kingdom. Nowhere is this more obviously apparent than in the constitutional history of the state. The very fact that the state, whose name according to its Constitution is 'Eire, or in the English language, Ireland' does not embrace the whole island of Ireland, immediately calls for explanation and is only explicable in terms of British actions and attitudes. The same is true of many other facts of Irish life.

Not surprisingly *Bunreacht na hEireann (Constitution of Ireland)*, 1937, the basic law of the state, is best understood as a stage in the evolution of Ireland's relationship with the United Kingdom, just as its predecessors, the Constitution of Dáil Eireann (1919) and the Constitution of the Irish Free State (1922) marked earlier stages. All were the products of the same process of national emancipation from British domination and influence. Although political independence was substantially effected in 1922, this fact was not crystal clear to many people, for the Constitution that embodied independence maintained the traditional British symbolic linkages involving the Crown and membership of the British Commonwealth. In any case, that independence extended to only twenty-six of the thirty-two counties of Ireland. These were the best terms that could be got from the United Kingdom at that time. Inevitably, the British insistence on those terms and British attitudes to the Irish desire to alter them became and remained the most important factor in determining Irish government policy over a wide range of issues and obsessed the Irish community as a whole. To a degree they continue to do so to this day.

Furthermore, political independence did not mean that the new state started with a blank sheet: far from it. To begin with, the political legacy of the departing imperial power in the shape of traditions, habits and institutions as well as patterns and levels of public services was enormous and could not be wiped out by a treaty leading to the emergence of a new sovereign state. Again, although political independence meant that the new state, the Irish Free State, was centred on Dublin, its capital, it took much longer for economic life to become Dublin oriented rather than London oriented and for the cultural life of the country to emerge from equivocal provincialism to a more wholesale Irishness.

Although this process was largely completed within half a century, a study of Irish constitutional politics has still to start with an examination of the impact of British policy and British attitudes generally in the face of Irish nationalist pressure to complete the job that was left unfinished in 1921-22. Even were this achieved with a satisfactory solution of the Northern Ireland problem, geography and history will continue to ensure that the British connection will always be an important factor in Irish life. The British and the Irish are more closely connected with each other than either is to any other group.

II

Ireland, like Scotland and Wales, was absorbed by the English and became and remained for centuries a province of an essentially English state. The coming of an absolutist regime in that state at the end of the medieval period meant the imposition of considerable uniformity. English control involved not simply political domination but social, economic and cultural domination also. In theory, if not always in fact, the peripheral regions of this state were not colonies but integral parts of what came to be called 'the United Kingdom of Great Britain and Ireland'. The process was formally completed by the Act of Union (1800).

The absorption of Ireland into an English-dominated society was aided by the practice of dispossessing the indigenous population of their land and transferring it to settlers who were English or Scottish in origin and Protestant in religion. This process produced a class of Protestant landowners who constituted a distinct sub-culture and there grew up an elite who dominated the island until the late nineteenth century. They and those better-off Catholics who associated themselves with them gave their allegiance to the British Crown and looked to London as their metropolis, just as did their counterparts in Scotland and Wales.

At this time, too, the essentially English United Kingdom attained the status of a world power with a vast empire centred on London which became not only a great political capital but a world financial, economic, communications and cultural centre as well. The people of this highly successful country had complete confidence in the excellence of all things English and a firm belief in the need for the peripheral peoples — the Welsh, the Scots, and the Irish — in their own interests to speak English, absorb English beliefs, adopt English habits and generally to identify with English traditions.

This process of absorption of English culture extended to political values, traditions and patterns of behaviour and was still continuing in the second half of the nineteenth century at the critical formative period of modern mass democracy. Extensions of the franchise (the right to vote) in Ireland were made step by step following upon those in Great Britain, and Irish politicians operated in the electoral, parliamentary and local government contexts of the British system. Public services were installed and developed to a great extent in parallel with those in Great Britain. In particular, compulsory primary education was extended to Ireland as to the mainland and this led to high levels of literacy at about the same time. Irish people developed liberal-democratic values and concepts of rights and duties similar to those of the British and looked upon both the political practices and the patterns and levels of public service of the British system as the norms.

Although, with the emergence of Sinn Féin, the Irish nationalist movement forsook constitutional methods in favour of direct action, the majority of its leaders believed in parliamentary democracy. They felt it necessary to make and seek acceptance for a constitution, the Constitution of Dáil Eireann, to establish the legitimacy of their republic, and '[its] political, constitutional and legal underpinnings were nurtured as carefully, perhaps more carefully, than the demands and occasional local claims of fighting men in the field.'[1]

As with their leaders, so too with Irish people generally. Despite the split in Sinn Féin and the subsequent civil war, there was widespread recognition of the legitimacy of the Pro-Treaty government simply because it was the only elected government. Subsequently, de Valera and his colleagues who had refused to recognize that government were fully legitimized when they in their turn finally espoused parliamentary methods. It was even more significant, as Frank Munger has pointed out, that eventually 'the government that had defeated de Valera in the field permitted him to triumph through the ballot.' As he observed, 'from our present acquaintance with political processes in new nations, we know how strange these events are. What seemed to the Irish natural, normal, even inevitable, has occurred in few other places.'[2]

Furthermore, it was a marked feature of the Irish experience that these values 'were articulated in a distinctively British way.'[3] The governmental institutions, devices and practices that were adopted were those in use in the United Kingdom, the Westminster and Whitehall models. The articles in the Irish Free State Constitution that dealt with the machinery of government were 'a bold attempt to capture the essential elements of cabinet government and squeeze them into the phraseology of constitutional clauses.'[4] Once installed, this early-twentieth-century-Westminster model, as it might appropriately be called, survived the stresses and strains of the first decade of independence which, it is now often forgotten, were considerable. Significantly, it was the 'un-British' provisions of the Irish Free State Constitution (those that provided for referenda, the initiative, and extern ministers) which were intended to modify the rigour of the British system, that were all removed. The marked tendency from the beginning to work the British system in undiluted form was confirmed when de Valera assumed office. Evidently, it could also accommodate his very different style of government. Although his Constitution, Bunreacht na hEireann, involved a radical revision of the constitutional status of the state and its relationships with the British Crown and Commonwealth, it largely confirmed what already existed so far as the machinery of government was concerned. The continuity between the two Constitutions in respect of the machinery and procedures of government was most marked, the very wording of some articles of *Bunreacht na hEireann* being nearly identical with that of its predecessor. Significantly, also, the civil service which had been taken over and retained intact in 1922 was hardly affected by the crucial political change of 1932: neither in 1922 nor 1932 was there a purge of the public service or a spate of political appointments.

Although in recent years the effectiveness of parliamentary and administrative systems and the whole apparatus of local government have come under increasing criticism, there have been few if any major reforms. The system of parliamentary committees instituted in 1983 has considerable potential, but many of the more radical changes in the administration advocated in the Report of the Public Services Organisation Review Group (1969) were still not made by 1991, nor had the often heralded reform of local government taken place. In both these areas government after government either shirked the issues or tinkered at the edges of the governmental machine. Ireland is still a country operating the Westminster and Whitehall models which have now become 'internalised'. In this respect it is recognizably in the British Commonwealth tradition.

III

The impact of the British connection on Irish politics as we have traced it so far has been largely positive. The Irish absorbed — admittedly willy-nilly — British political traditions and institutions as part of a general blanketing of Irish society by the British. However, British influence has also to be seen in the context of Irish nationalism and the demand for independence. Here the interaction has not been one of absorption but of rejection leading to conflict. In relation to the one remaining nationalist issue, Northern Ireland, that conflict continues to this day.

Ireland being more peripheral than Wales and Scotland was less assimilated into the United Kingdom. Important differences persisted to buttress the separate ethnic identities. These included religious differences and the survival of the remnants of the Gaelic culture and a pre-industrial peasant society after the English heartland had been transformed into an urban, industrial society. Nationalist leaders — most of them lower middle class and intellectuals — had a core mass support amongst rural peasant farming people with traditional instincts and loyalties.

The achievement of the independence movement in the shape of the Irish Free State was not seen as a complete success by anyone. To some, Pearse's words were sacred and to accept 'anything less by one fraction of one iota than separation from England' was an 'immense' crime:[5] to the more pragmatic like Michael Collins the Treaty might not have achieved 'the ultimate freedom that all nations desire', but it did give 'the freedom to achieve it'.[6] Consequently, the inevitable, nationalist self-consciousness, even touchiness, of the people of a newly independent small state next to a much bigger one was heightened in the Irish case, first, by the irritation of having to accept Commonwealth status which involved allegiance to the British Crown and, second, by the nagging irredentism caused by the existence of the border and 'the six counties'. To Irish leaders and public alike it was the British who had not only insisted upon the constitutional forms embodied in the Treaty and the Constitution which was a part of it, but who also had created the province of Northern Ireland, and thus a Northern Ireland problem.

These two sets of issues dominated Irish politics from the early twenties. One of them, that which concerned the constitutional status of the Irish state, was soluble and was eventually solved, though not until it had created a major cleavage among Irish leaders and activists that was to have a formative influence on politics and a corrosive effect on the whole society. The split of the independence movement over the terms of the Treaty, the civil war in which this issued, and the subsequent creation of the major parties reflecting this division are among the basic facts of Irish political history. Those parties have always conducted a highly adversarial kind of politics that has given Irish political behaviour one of its major characteristics. Clearly we cannot say that all this is due to British attitudes and policies: there is more to it than that. Equally clearly, these attitudes and policies did create a situation and made the occasion for the fundamental cleavage that dominated politics for so long.

Both the British imposition of the disputed constitutional linkages and the resolution of the issues which this posed are to be seen in successive constitutions and constitutional amendments. The links were broken one after another by legislation, in constitutional amendments and in *Bunreacht na hEireann*. Eventually, in 1948, the British acquiesced in the fact of an Irish republic outside the Commonwealth. In the very act of doing so, the British government — and no less so, the Irish government too — recognized the continued existence of a special relationship between the two countries. Prime Minister Clement Attlee's statement to the British House of Commons put the situation clearly:

> The Government regret that Eire will. . . no longer be a member of the Commonwealth. The Eire government, however, stated that they recognize the existence of a specially close relationship between Eire and the Commonwealth countries and desire that this relationship should be maintained. These close relations arise from ties of kinship and from traditional and long established economic, social and trade connections based on common interest. . .
>
> Accordingly the United Kingdom government will not regard the enactment of this legislation by Eire [the Republic of Ireland Act, 1948] as placing Eire in the category of foreign countries or Eire citizens in the category of foreigners.[7]

That 'specially close relationship' is reflected in legislation relating to such matters as nationality and citizenship, to safety at sea and in the air, and to entry to professions; in the cooperation of public authorities and other organizations; and in countless other ways.

These issues of constitutional forms and the status of the state were regarded by most Irish political leaders of the twenties and thirties as being of overriding importance and it was these that were the major cause of the split in Sinn Féin. The other problem, that of the partition of the island, was usually seen as insoluble in the short run at least and less immediately important. During the Treaty negotiations de Valera 'distinguished carefully between Ulster and "the big question", that of the crown.'[8] During the Treaty debates and after, 'Dáil Deputies, and later IRA members, had more interest in the status of the new Ireland than in its size.'[9] Of course, successive Irish governments demanded reunification, but although sometimes individual British ministers and governments seemed in principle willing to trade off Ulster for something that they regarded as more valuable, their room for manoeuvre was tightly circumscribed by the Ulster Unionists. However, many Southern leaders said — and some believed — that appropriate British action could lead to the creation of a thirty-two county

Irish state. They could always, and they did, blame the British for not initiating it. Despite the long delayed and only gradual public recognition of the real nature of the Northern problem, from the sixties onwards, some Irish leaders continue to express these views to this day.

As the constitutional issues were resolved from the late thirties onwards, the Northern Ireland problem came more and more to the centre. In the words of Michael Laffan, by 1938, 'the question of partition, virtually ignored in 1921-2, assumed a new importance.'[10] The wording of *Bunreacht na hEireann* reflected the Irish view well with Articles 2 and 3 enunciating the juridical claim to the whole island of Ireland and Article 3 recognizing as a practical necessity that 'pending the reintegration of the national territory' the jurisdiction of the state only extended to the twenty-six counties.

However, that Constitution reflected also a set of objectives aimed at by de Valera, Fianna Fáil and many, perhaps most, Irish people that were in fact contradictory and even mutually exclusive. To look for a Gaelic, Catholic, thirty-two county republic was to ask for the impossible given the presence of Northern Unionists. To the extent that a Gaelic, Catholic twenty-six-county republic was in the making, any hopes that there might have been of absorbing the other six counties were being dashed. Unionists would never accept it and neither the British government nor the Irish government — nor both in concert — could force them into such a state, nor into any all-Ireland polity, whatever its nature. Obvious as it may be now more than half a century later, this fact was evidently hardly recognized at the time.

Those who demand or propound solutions to this intransigent problem are of two types: they are either constitutionalists or proponents of direct action including armed force. The demands and suggested solutions of the first group, which includes both Irish and British, litter the pages of Irish constitutional history and are a constant theme of contemporary constitutional politics. Never more than now has the problem of Northern Ireland been coupled with issues of constitutional reform. The activities of the second group exacerbate the problems with which the first group are grappling. Although they can thwart possible constitutional solutions, as witness the fate of the so-called power-sharing Executive in May 1974 in the face of the direct action of the Ulster Workers' Council, they cannot alter the basic irreconcilable fundamentals of the situation of which they are a part.

IV

In contrast to the experience of third world countries, Irish independence involved the take-over, lock, stock and barrel, of a going concern by people well able to keep it going. Moreover, most of the leaders of the independence movement were not social revolutionaries: their goal was political independence not far-reaching socio-economic reforms. The framework of modern Ireland was already in place and it was retained with very little modification.

The Final Report of the Commission of Enquiry into the Civil Service, published not much more than a decade after the foundation of the state, described the impact of independence as follows:

> The passing of the state services into the control of a native government, however revolutionary it may have been as a step in the political development of the nation, entailed, broadly speaking, no immediate disturbance of any fundamental kind in the daily work of the average civil servant. Under changed masters the same main tasks of administration continued to be performed by the same staffs on the same general lines of organization and procedure. [11]

The same could have been said of many other facets of Irish life which changed only slowly if at all. It took decades for the financial and business worlds whose centre was London to reorient themselves upon Dublin. Even as recently as the early seventies over two thirds of Ireland's exports went to the United Kingdom and half its imports came from there. It was only in 1979 that the Irish pound ceased to be linked in a one-to-one relationship with the pound sterling.

The flow of information between the two islands underpinned the ties. Because of the proximity of the Republic of Ireland with its three and a half million English-speaking people to a market of sixty million British people, the cultural influence of Britain has always been and remains immense. Obviously Irish publishers have been severely handicapped: evidently, also, Irish broadcasting has been constrained in circumstances where virtually everyone has access to British radio programmes and where most television sets can receive British programmes. In the light of this, the considerable emulation effect that has been so evident in Irish life is inevitable, the more so because of the high levels of emigration from Ireland to Britain in the past and the constant coming and going — on holiday, to get work or training, to have an expensive operation

on the British National Health Service, or for whatever purpose.
Most of this has had no direct bearing upon the Constitution but
it has created a climate of opinion and expectations, a context within
which political issues, including some with constitutional
implications, are debated.

Recently, however, the context has been changing. Until the
early seventies, Ireland was seen by Europeans as 'une île derrière
une île'[12], blanketed and insulated by Great Britain. Ireland's view
of continental Europe was reciprocal. With Ireland's accession to
the European Communities, the position began to change quite
quickly. The intrusion of Community law into Ireland and the impact
of a flow of Community funds has led to a substitution of Community
influence for British. The imperatives of membership have had
considerable effects and this is only the beginning.

In the debate on Irish accession to the Communities, Garret
FitzGerald advocated membership because it would lessen Irish
dependence on Britain in trade and would strengthen the Irish voice
against the British at inter-governmental level. Irish experience of
membership shows that the impact is much wider than this, and
in some areas is irresistible. Accession itself required a constitutional
amendment and so did ratification of the Single European Act.
In each case only minimal changes were made but many more are
needed to bring the Constitution into line with Community law
and make it internally consistent. The potential impact upon the
rights of Irish people of the Community Treaties and their
interpretation by the European Court of Justice is immense. Rights
that are apparently enshrined in the Constitution are being
interpreted by that Court and some might even have to be amended.
Conversely, other conditions of life and work which are not legal
rights in Irish domestic law might well be so in Community law.
Community membership has, too, raised the issues of sovereignty
and neutrality that are highly emotive in a new context. They must
now be seen in a European and not the traditional, narrow Anglo-
Irish setting.

More widely, the effects of the Treaties and of the activities
of the various Community institutions upon patterns of economic
activity and of public services are becoming daily more pervasive.
As we shall see, by virtue of membership of the Communities, Ireland
has in effect two constitutions, two sources of law and two centres
of political and administrative decision making, one in Dublin, the

other in Brussels. In these circumstances, the influence of the British connection will be progressively diluted in the future: as yet, however, this process is still only in its early stages.

— 3 —

De Valera and
the Constitution

BUNREACHT NA hEIREANN was de Valera's Constitution. In it, he sought so far as he could to embody his principles, to reflect his experience of how to conduct government, and to realize his vision of an ideal Irish society. In this respect it differed from the constitution which it replaced, for the Irish Free State Constitution was the product of a negotiated treaty and reflected compromises between republican nationalist demands and the constitutional principles of the British Commonwealth.

It was these compromises that had driven de Valera and his followers into opposition and civil war. Consequently, his accession to office was the occasion for a new constitution. Although the Cumann na nGaedheal governments which were in power for the first decade of independence had no hesitation in amending the machinery-of-government articles of the Irish Free State Constitution as necessity, experience, or convenience dictated, when it came to provisions concerning the status of the state, Commonwealth membership, the monarchy and the oath, they felt bound by the Treaty and the Constitution as enacted. These were precisely the provisions de Valera was pledged to remove. Their erasure involved, firstly, a series of amendments to the Irish Free State Constitution to remove offending articles; secondly, taking an unexpected opportunity with the crisis that led to the abdication of Edward VIII in 1936, the removal of references to the Crown in the Constitution; and, thirdly, the making of a new constitution. 'The new constitution ... marked the culmination of a fifteen-year campaign against the Treaty. Its purpose was to destroy that

20

settlement, justify de Valera's constitutional opposition to it, and positively to vest the state's sovereignty in the people...'[1]. That it also offered the opportunity to effect changes in the machinery of government and to make ideological declarations and statements of rights and duties of a more indigenous, i.e. Catholic and Irish, character, however welcome or necessary, was of secondary importance.

The extent to which *Bunreacht na hEireann* was the brain child of de Valera can have few parallels in the history of constitution making. He personally presided over its preparation and drafting. Where provisions of the Irish Free State Constitution were unobjectionable, he retained them, sometimes with little change. Although principles were agreed in government and some of his colleagues offered observations on particular articles at the draft stage, it was very much his personal project and they left it to him. He had the help of a number of civil servants, principally John Hearne, legal adviser to the Department of External Affairs, who did much of the actual work on the draft and who might also have had some influence upon its content.[2] Hearne and three other civil servants comprised a committee of officials whose job it was to prepare material for consideration and decision. There were also committees to handle the problems of translating the English drafts into Irish. In addition, de Valera sought observations from departments on draft articles relevant to their activities. He also consulted a few outsiders, notably a number of Catholic clergy, on the rights and social principles articles and some of them submitted material and drafts to him. He tried out his drafts of Article 44 (on religion) on church leaders of a number of denominations.[3]

Once the Constitution was drafted, he completely identified himself with it. He personally presented it to the people (in a radio broadcast) and to the Dáil (the Senate had been abolished and no second chamber existed at that time). He piloted it through the Dáil virtually single-handed, explaining and defending its provisions, where necessary sentence by sentence, word by word; and he campaigned for it in the referendum that he deemed necessary for its enactment. This was certainly de Valera's Constitution: it does not follow that its provisions were all he would have wished.

In the ideal world of de Valera, the constitution of his country would have been unequivocally republican; it would have applied to the whole island; and it would have been Catholic and Gaelic. It would also have attempted to foster the values of the rural, peasant population of a mythical Irish 'golden age' which sometimes at least he appeared to believe had actually existed. Certainly, these aspirations are all evident but, politician as he was, he recognised the context within which he was operating and appreciated the dilemma he faced in regard to the nationalist demand to include Northern Unionists in an all-Ireland state. That he was in a position to write his country's fundamental law did not signal final victory for his cause. It marked a stage, albeit an important one, in what was to prove a life-long struggle, in John Bowman's words, 'to [reconcile], on the one hand, the aspiration to an independent, sovereign, separatist republic for the entire island of Ireland, with, on the other, his appreciation that, strategically, Irish defence was inseparable from that of Britain, and that in the north-east of the island, a local majority was determined to resist Irish unity on the nationalists' terms.'[4]

II

Bunreacht na hEireann was designed to be a constitution for an Irish Republic. To make the point clearly and unequivocally and in an effort to appease or undermine the fundamentalists who would not recognise the existing regime, it was to be enacted by the people. In his radio broadcast, de Valera told his listeners that 'sovereignty resides in them the people as their inalienable and indefeasible right', and in the Preamble of the Constitution the point is explicitly made: 'We, the people of Eire, ... do hereby adopt, enact, and give to ourselves this Constitution'.

In declaring the people to be the source of all authority in the state, de Valera was destroying Commonwealth status and tearing up the Treaty, and this was his intention. He was also making the country a republic, for a republic is by definition — a definition that he was himself to use in the famous 'dictionary republic' debate — 'a state in which supreme power rests in the people and their elected representatives or officers, as opposed to one governed by a king or the like....'[5] Republics usually have presidents and *Bunreacht na hEireann* duly provided for a popularly elected

President of Ireland.[6] However, nowhere in this unilateral declaration of a republic — for that is what the Constitution was, did it actually state that the country was a republic. Instead, Article 5 declares that 'Ireland is a sovereign, independent, democratic state.'

The omission was deliberate. Consistently from 1921 when he had put forward 'Document No. 2' as his alternative to the Treaty, de Valera recognised the element of inconsistency in nationalist aspirations. To go to the ultimate in pursuing the goal of a separate state i.e. refusing to recognise the British monarchy altogether and declaring a republic, would be to jettison any hope of inducing Northern Unionists to come into an all-Ireland state; and, notwithstanding anything that was said for propaganda purposes or public morale, they could not be forced in. De Valera was explicit on the point during the Dáil debates on the draft Constitution. 'If the Northern problem were not there... in all probability there would be a flat downright proclamation of a republic....'[7] His policy of 'external association' enunciated in Document No. 2 during the Treaty debate in December 1921 and January 1922 became and remained his answer to this dilemma.

Central to Document No. 2 was the proposal 'that for purposes of common concern, Ireland shall be associated with the states of the British Commonwealth... that the matters of "common concern" shall include Defence, Peace and War, Political Treaties, and all matters now treated as of common concern, amongst the States of the British Commonwealth... [and] that, for purposes of the Association, Ireland shall recognise his Britannic Majesty as head of the Association.'[8] At the abdication of King Edward VIII in 1936, this policy was reflected in the arrangement by which the crown was removed from the Irish Free State Constitution by amendment and reintroduced by statute solely for the purposes of appointing diplomatic and consular representatives and making international agreements.[9] In *Bunreacht na hEireann* (in Article 29.4.2[0]) provision is made for continuing these arrangements, though the language used is more obscure and less felicitous:

> For the purpose of the exercise of any executive function of the State in or in connection with its external relations, the government may to such extent and subject to such conditions, if any, as may be determined by law, avail of or adopt any organ, instrument, or method of procedure used or adopted for the like purpose by the members of any group or league

of nations with which the state is or becomes associated for the purpose of international cooperation in matters of common concern.

From 29 December 1937, the day on which *Bunreacht na hEireann* came into force, the Irish state (now widely to be called Eire, the Irish name given to it in the Constitution itself) was effectively no longer a member of the British Commonwealth, and the British crown was made use of only for accrediting diplomatic representatives. However, neither the British government of the day nor Commonwealth governments accepted that any change in the status of the Irish state had been effected by the Constitution and there followed a decade of ambiguity about it. De Valera did little to attempt to dispel it. See, for example, his answer to 'Deputy Dillon's second question' in the so-called 'dictionary republic' debate: 'that is a question for which the material necessary for a conclusive answer is not fully available,' he said, and proceeded to add a few paragraphs of 'material' of his own that could not but make the position even more obscure.[10] Deliberately so, for he was trying as always to keep open 'a bridge over which the Northern Unionists might one day walk.'[11] His decision not to declare that the state was a republic and his formulations in the Constitution, he said, 'puts the question of our international relations in their proper place and that is outside the Constitution.'[12] Not one word of the Constitution would have to be changed to break the links and declare the state formally a republic, if and when it became advantageous to do so.

When in 1948 a coalition government of his political opponents led by John A. Costello did decide to do so, a single short statute, the Republic of Ireland Act, 1948, was all that was necessary. That act repeated the External Relations Act, assigned all executive power to the President acting on the advice of the government, and declared that 'the description of the state shall be the Republic of Ireland.' The position was at last tidied up, and made the more tidy by the governments of the United Kingdom and Commonwealth countries now acknowledging formally that Ireland was, indeed, no longer a member of the Commonwealth.

The declaration of a republic was effected, as we have noted, not by de Valera but by his political opponents. Once it was mooted, however, 'he promised no opposition from the Fianna Fáil benches.'[13] He could hardly do anything else but, according to John

Bowman, 'it should not be assumed ... that the decision met with his approval' for, as he told an official biographer, Frank Gallagher, 'he believed harm would come to the cause of unity from the bridge to the North East being destroyed.'[14] No wonder he was, as Gallagher put it, 'troubled', for external association, his preferred policy, seemed to have been made more difficult. Northern Unionist intransigence was certainly strengthened by the guarantee contained in the Ireland Act, 1949, which was Britain's riposte.

As so often in Anglo-Irish dealings on independence, a significant advance on one front only worsened the position on the other. The declaration of the republic was no exception for it lessened, or at the very least deferred, whatever chance there might have been of making any progress on the partition issue. The situation was very familiar to de Valera. Time and again from the Treaty negotiations onwards, he recognised and faced up to the impossibility of soon attaining the goal of a united Ireland. Certainly every opportunity had to be taken to raise the issue, but other more attainable objectives had priority. Partition was constantly placed 'on the back burner'. His treatment of it in *Bunreacht na hEireann* — the juridical claim in Article 2 to the whole island and the de facto recognition in Article 3 of the reality of the situation — reflected this view and this strategy. So, too, did his willingness to drop the partition issue in the negotiations leading up to the Anglo-Irish agreement of 1938 in return for the Treaty ports. Likewise, during World War II he rejected a British offer to trade a declaration of acceptance of the principle of a united Ireland for the abandonment of neutrality if the Northern government could be cajoled into agreement.

The last decade of de Valera's career in active politics was, in John Bowman's words, 'an inauspicious period'.[15] As always, he continued to deflect the impatient in his own party. His attitude to the more active anti-partition policies of the coalition governments which supplanted him for two three-year periods between 1948 and 1957 was grudging. He 'invariably seemed more willing than other nationalists to admit the intractability of the partition problem' and he reckoned that 'nothing better than a policy of patience and opportunism was possible.'[16] With Seán Lemass, his successor now waiting in the wings, he increasingly inclined to the view that 'the proper way to try to solve it was to endeavour to have as close relations as possible with the people of the six counties and get them to combine with us on matters of common concern.'[17] Partition was once again on the back burner.

III

The incompatibility of de Valera's nationalist aspirations was not simply a matter for him to resolve within his own mind — if he could — and to decide what his own priorities were. He could not compromise on the basic aims of his movement, however irreconcilable, much more than he did and still maintain his support in his own party. He himself constantly made this point to his British contacts and it was true. The same probably cannot be said for what John Bowman termed 'optional extras' in [his] programme, 'to which he was personally committed, but to which many of his cabinet colleagues were indifferent, ambivalent or hostile, and which served further to alienate the Ulster Unionists.'[18] His treatment of the Roman Catholic religion and values and his insistence on giving priority to the Irish language are examples in *Bunreacht na hEireann.*

The Jrish Free State Constitution reflected the liberal tradition and liberal values as they had evolved in Britain. The rights which it guaranteed included personal rights such as habeas corpus, freedom to practise any religion, freedom of association and the inviolability of the citizen's home, altogether a classic traditional liberal list. In order to allay Protestant fears, that Constitution also deliberately inclined to secular indifference. The state was prohibited from endowing any religion, from discrimination on account of religious belief and from acquiring church property by compulsion, except for certain enumerated public works and then only on payment of compensation.

In practice, the Cumann na nGaedheal government 'proved willing to use the power of the State to protect Catholic moral values.'[19] Fianna Fáil in its turn followed suit. In his book *Church and State in Modern Ireland 1923–1979,* John Whyte entitles the chapter on the period 1923–37 'The Catholic moral code becomes enshrined in the law of the state.' This was not a matter of bowing to church pressure: there was no need for that at that time since 'ministers were products of the same culture as the bishops, and shared the same values.'[20] In particular, de Valera himself 'was a devout Catholic of conservative religious views.'[21] Moreover, he was inclined at times to equate 'Irish' with 'Catholic' and to ignore or reject the non-Catholic people:

> Since the coming of St. Patrick, fifteen hundred years ago, Ireland has been a Christian and a Catholic nation. All the ruthless attempts made down through the centuries to force her from this allegiance have not shaken her faith. She remains a Catholic nation.[22]

Like the Cumann na nGaedheal government which he succeeded, he, too, was prepared to legislate to enforce Catholic moral standards, and *Bunreacht na hEireann* was, in Whyte's words, 'the coping stone of this development'.[23]

The influence of contemporary Catholic teaching was to be seen particularly in some of the rights articles, and in Article 45 entitled 'Directive Principles of Social Policy'. Elsewhere, the enthusiasm of Catholic writers of the time for vocationalism that was advocated in the Encyclical *Quadragesimo Anno* of Pope Pius XI was reflected in Articles 18 and 19 which dealt with the composition of Seanad Eireann (the Senate) and provided for vocational representation, and in Article 15.3.1^0 (on the National Parliament) which permitted the establishment and recognition of functional or vocational councils representing branches of the social and economic life of the people.

Given the context and tone of Catholic social teaching in the thirties and the distinct air of triumphalism amongst the Irish clergy at that time, it was, as Garret FitzGerald has pointed out, 'an unfortunate period in history to be drawing it [the Constitution] up because it was a period when a strong view was held that a Constitution should incorporate ideas emanating from a particular church. This view wouldn't have been held twenty years earlier or say twenty to thirty years later'.[24] It was Article 44 (on religion) in particular that was to raise the major problem of reconciling three diverse traditions — the liberal principles inherited from the Irish Free State Constitution, Northern fears that 'home rule is Rome rule' and the prevailing Catholic view about the duty of the state in respect of religion.

Writing about the making of the Constitution, de Valera's biographers note that he 'was to admit later that Article 44 gave him more anxiety than anything else in [it]'.[25] The difficulty he faced in reconciling his objectives was obvious and it was over this article that the pressures and interests which he was seeking to reconcile were most evident. He consulted a number of senior clergy including the Papal Nuncio, (Paschal Robinson), and the Cardinal Archbishop of Armagh (Cardinal MacRory). The Pope himself was secretly shown a draft of the whole Constitution. However, the final draft was de Valera's own.[26] In Article 44.1.2^0 as enacted:

> the State recognises the special position of the Holy Catholic Apostolic and Roman Church as the guardian of the Faith professed by the great majority of the citizens.

Recognition was also accorded to other religious denominations that existed in the country at the time and the Article contained assurances on freedom of conscience and the free profession and practice of religion. In addition, following the terms of Article 8 of the Irish Free State Constitution, the state guaranteed not to endow any religion, not to impose disabilities on religious grounds, not to discriminate in providing aid for schools and not to interfere with church property compulsorily except for 'necessary works of public utility and on payment of compensation'.

As far as Catholic teaching of the time was concerned, de Valera's attempt to produce a formulation, as his biographers put it, 'better suited to Irish conditions',[27] was less than ideal. At that time, the Church maintained that it was the duty of rulers to make a public profession of religion and to support it, in the words of the Encyclical *Immortale Dei*, 'not such religion as they may have preference for, but the religion which God enjoins, and which certain and most clear marks show to be the only one true religion.'[28] The extent of the compromise de Valera was making is perhaps best appreciated if the wording of Article 44.1.2^0 as it finally emerged (which is quoted above) is compared with earlier drafts in the files in the State Paper Office. The preliminary draft of this Article ran as follows:

> The State acknowledges that the true religion is that established by our Divine Lord, Jesus Christ Himself, which he committed to his Church to protect and propagate, as the guardian and interpreter of true morality. It acknowledges, moreover, that the Church of Christ is the Catholic Church.[29]

For all de Valera's efforts and despite the fact that the leaders of the other churches in the state found his formulation acceptable,

Article 44 was yet another provision of Bunreacht na hEireann that further hardened the opposition of Northern Protestants to any connection with the South. As Conor Cruise O'Brien put it:

> ... if indeed he was interested in wooing "the North" — in practice, the Protestants of Northern Ireland — his Constitution of 1937 was an odd bouquet to choose.
>
> Article 2 of the Constitution declared the national territory to be 'the whole island of Ireland, its islands and the territorial seas'.
>
> Article 3 asserted — while leaving in suspense for the time being — "the right of the Parliament and government established by this Constitution to exercise jurisdiction over the whole of that territory".
>
> Article 44.1.2 recognized "the special position of the Holy Catholic Apostolic and Roman church as the guardian of the Faith professed by the great majority of the citizens".
>
> Thus, the Protestants of Northern Ireland were declared incorporated de jure into a State which recognized the special position of the Roman Catholic Church. It would be hard to think of a combination of propositions more likely to sustain and stiffen the siege-mentality of Protestant Ulster.[30]

IV

Conor Cruise O'Brien's catalogue might well have included yet another item, the status accorded to the Irish language. The language was one of two issues which, according to de Valera himself, had drawn him into public life (the other was the threat of partition). Indeed, 'of the two, the Irish language was, he thought, the more urgent.'[31] Sometimes he went so far as to say that he would abandon the goal of a united Ireland if that necessitated abandoning the language.[32] If Irish, a language which incidentally he learned in his middle twenties, were to disappear so, too, in his view would Irish nationality. Although he aspired to an Irish-speaking nation, according to his biographers he accepted that both Irish and English would be necessary, 'with Irish as the home language, while English remained the language which gives most ready access to the outside world'[33]

The occasion of *Bunreacht na hEireann* gave him an opportunity to forward his aspirations: in fact he did not go very far. In Article 8 the Irish language as 'the national language' was declared to be 'the first official language' with English 'recognised as a second official language'. In cases of conflict between the two texts of a law, 'the text in the national language shall prevail.' Under Article 8, also, 'provision may ... be made by law for the exclusive use of either of the said languages for any one or more official purposes....' Unless he and his government were prepared to take draconian measures — as governments elsewhere have sometimes done — that was as far as he could realistically go, for as he sadly told his biographers years later, 'the nation as a whole had not yet put its back into it.'[34]

To Northern Unionists the language policies of Irish governments were regarded as fantasy, 'a sort of awful insanity', according to Hugh Shearman a decade later.[35] Yet Longford and O'Neill record de Valera later in life as having:

> no fear that his dream of restoring Irish would run counter in any way to his other dream — the reuniting of the country. His view would be that the Northern Unionists were, at bottom, proud of being Irish; that the history, tradition and culture of the historic Irish nation could not fail to attract them; that the language was a mine of this tradition and culture .... [36]

In this as in other matters also, it is painfully obvious that de Valera did not really understand the North.[37]

V

Judged as a constitution for the state that actually existed i.e. the twenty-six county state, de Valera's creation was a great success. It quickly became and remained a 'normative' constitution in Loewenstein's sense of the term (see above, p. 6), 'a suit that fits and that is actually worn'. That very congruence, however, inevitably meant that it was not a satisfactory constitution for a country comprising the whole island: on the contrary, it offended deeply-held convictions of some Northerners and hardened their opposition ...alist aspirations. In John Bowman's judgement:

the 1937 Constitution was the most formal expression of the contradiction at the core of Fianna Fáil's strategy on unification: their attempt at nation-building on a specifically republican, Catholic, Gaelic model in an island where such values were not shared or tolerable throughout the putative nation.[38]

Half a century later this view is coming to be widely accepted in the Republic. It is the more important, therefore, to notice that it was not generally perceived at the time in the twenty-six countries. De Valera certainly recognized that he faced a problem, but, as he saw it, it was a problem of getting consent. He constantly justified the compromises he made and the stands he took by reference to the extremists in his own party or to Irish opinion generally, the implication being that he would, if he could, have gone further. What he did not see was that nationalist objectives were irreconcilably contradictory, let alone that one of them, an all-Ireland state, might be for ever unattainable because Unionists would never agree to it under any circumstances. Many people in the Republic are not prepared to contemplate this even today let alone in the late thirties.

De Valera himself was very evidently satisfied with his handiwork. He saw *Bunreacht na hEireann* as a finished product and although, during its passage through the Dáil, he sometimes defended particular clauses as having been drafted to meet the precise needs of the situation at that time, he evidently did not envisage a process of constant constitutional development. De Valera's view was reinforced by the absence of any complaints about the Constitution from the public generally once the party wrangling during its passage through the Dáil was over. Virtually the only calls for amendment came from women's groups over the role of women envisaged in the Constitution and from extreme Catholic groups seeking to have the troublesome Article 44 strengthened. As a result there followed a period of constitutional stagnation. Nothing flowed through either of the constitutional channels for development. The legislature approved no constitutional amendments after the initial tidying-up period because de Valera himself was in office for so long and so continuously, and there was in any case no demand from a thoroughly conservative public: the courts delivered no judgements of a positive or developmental kind because the judges, being unused to having the power of review and unwilling to invalidate governmental or parliamentary action on constitutional grounds, were cautious even inhibited in their approach.

It was not until de Valera had retired from active politics and Ireland was changing very rapidly in an era of industrialisation and urbanization, that his successors, Lemass and Lynch, began to contemplate new initiatives on the North and to face up to the need to adapt Irish institutions to changing social pressures. The fate of their efforts is instructive. A proposal in the Report of the 1967 Committee on the Constitution in respect of Article 3 was condemned as heresy by traditionalists in Fianna Fáil and was received with apathy by a public that had not been prepared by the politicians for change. Similarly, Lynch's effort to modify party policy on the North was one of the causes of the internal dissension that racked Fianna Fáil from 1970 onwards. Likewise, although the more ecumenical attitude of the Church in the post Vatican II period of *aggiornamento* permitted the deletion of the 'special position' clause in Article 44 in 1972, that was the limit of reform so far as Irish bishops were concerned. As they contemplated a growing demand for the state to amend the Constitution or to legislate to permit divorce, abortion and the sale of contraceptives, their fears of the domino effect of liberalizing reforms led them to favour a tenacious rearguard action against change.

Thus, the experience of those who have attempted to change de Valera's Constitution is instructive, even chastening. To this day, proponents of constitutional amendment face formidable opposition. It comes first, from the fundamentalists in Fianna Fáil who regard *Bunreacht na hEireann* as de Valera's legacy to his movement and the embodiment of Fianna Fáil's original aims in so far as they can be realised. It comes, second, from campaigners in the name of, or at the behest of, the Catholic Church, as they attempt to hold a line on a number of matters of conscience — their consciences at least. Clearly, 'the Chief' still casts long shadows. To this day, when we speak of de Valera and the Constitution, we are not just talking history; we are talking politics.

—— 4 ——

The Church and
the Constitution

BUNREACHT NA hEIREANN, de Valera's Constitution, was in the words of his long-serving first lieutenant, Seán T. Ó Ceallaigh, 'worthy of a catholic country'.[1] Although some of de Valera's other colleagues might not have gone so far down that road, he did in fact accurately reflect the values of the vast majority of the people of the twenty-six counties. It is true that there was political warfare over the draft constitution which was eventually approved in a referendum by only fifty-one per cent of those voting, but this was because it raised issues like Commonwealth status and the Treaty: in respect of matters where the Church had an interest, there was virtual consensus in the country. The procedures followed by de Valera in drafting the Constitution, which involved consultation with clerics and clearance from the Vatican on matters which concerned the Church, were thoroughly in keeping with the cultural climate of the twenty-six counties at that time. To a large extent so, too, was its content.

In his book entitled *A General Theory of Secularization,* David Martin notes that:

> an indissoluble union of church and nation arises in those situations where the church has been the sole available vehicle of nationality against foreign domination: Greece, Cyprus, Poland, Belgium, Ireland, Croatia. . . . The countries mentioned remain areas of high practice and belief. . . . The myth of identity is strengthened further wherever the dominated group have been at the border with another faith. . . .[2]

He contends that in such societies 'the historic role of the church as guardian of a culture. . . leads to the accession of further roles and these are carried forward with the onset of independence and/ or industrialisation.'[3] In such countries the status of the clergy is high and anti-clericalism low. The relationship between state and church remains intimate, for the state supports the religion and there is agreement between church and state over fundamental values. The church plays an important cultural role and church activities are wide-ranging: in particular, it strongly influences the education system.

In Martin's view the universal tendency of societies to become secularized, which is the consequence of industrialization, urbanization and greater geographical and social mobility, is impeded and slowed down by the tenacity of religion in such societies. They remain, as he says, 'areas of high practice and belief'. This does not apply only to Catholic societies: 'As Ireland illustrates, King William's defeat of the Irish at the Boyne is part of contemporary reality. Like the candles it still burns.'[4]

The features that Martin identifies were very evident in the development of the Irish state in its first years, not least in constitutional development. Likewise, although from the 1960s the conditions that promote secularization began to manifest themselves strongly in Ireland, the development of secular attitudes and responses was slow and the hold of religion tenacious, as he hypothesized. In the words of Liam Ryan, writing in 1984, 'the old order was challenged but not destroyed, it wilted but did not wither.'[5]

II

The consensus in the new twenty-six county state which permitted the considerable catholicization of state and community institutions alike, prevailed for almost half a century, from its foundation into the sixties. The circumstances could hardly have been more propitious for it. Because of partition, the population of the new state was overwhelmingly Catholic — 93 per cent in 1926; 95 per cent in 1961 — a people moreover devoutly Catholic and accustomed to the paternalistic control of their clergy. Consonant with David Martin's 'nationalist' model of secularization the identification in the public mind of the church with the national movement and independence boosted religion in people's scale of values and affection and thus retarded the process. Because Catholic values were internalized in the community, and because the church's control of education ensured that this persisted from generation to generation, the views and attitudes of the clergy — in practice, given the kind of church it was, of the bishops who comprised 'the Hierarchy' — generally prevailed in most matters in which they took an interest.

The Irish clergy's view of the proper relationship between society, the Catholic church and the state; of the duty of the state towards the church; and of the position to be accorded to other religions were some way from those that prevailed generally in the pluralist democracies of Western Europe and North America. However, the fact that in general Irish people accepted liberal-democratic values deriving from the British tradition prevented the new state from developing into a right-wing Catholic, authoritarian regime. Although de Valera occasionally proposed that Unionists, who were of course Protestants, should get out if they did not like what was on offer, he nevertheless included members of religions other than Catholicism in his Ireland and, as we have seen, went to considerable lengths to consult and accommodate the views of their leaders when he was drafting his Constitution. For its part, the Catholic Church would have been quite happy had he taken a more rigid line, for its demeanour at this time inclined to a conservative authoritarianism that suited its role as a folk church geared to the needs and limitations of a largely rural, peasant people.

As the brief excursion of the Vatican and Catholic publicists generally into vocationalism in the nineteen-thirties demonstrated, the Church generally was also 'integralist'. Characterising this stance, John Hickey explained it as follows:

> Ideally, the Church must attempt to permeate all the other institutions in society; and not just permeate but, if possible, control them so that the society itself becomes a place wherein not only is the *Depositum Fidei* preserved but its social potential idealized and the City of God achieved.
>
> This, in turn means control; control not just of the committed members of the Church but also of the means by which the whole society regulates itself — that is the political institution (government), the family institution (which provides the socialization for future members of the society), the educational institution (experienced now in the formal school system) and the economic institution.[6]

From the twenties a *de facto* established church and from December 1937 having *de jure* a 'special position', the Catholic church in the twenty-six counties was well on the road to this objective so far as the political situation was concerned.

Although the Church was not formally accorded the status of an established church, it was because it did not need to be: if there was no specifically Catholic political party, it was because there was no call for one: if the clergy only intervened overtly in politics very occasionally, it was because there was no necessity for it. In areas in which it had an interest — education, family law, health — those charged with formulating and administering policy approached their task imbued with the basic values of their Church. If politicians or public servants needed guidance or thought it politic to seek it from the clergy, they could, and did, do so quietly and sometimes covertly. For their part, the bishops could, and did, expect to be consulted and to have their advice followed. Where questions of moral and even social right and wrong or of rights as defined by the Church were concerned, they saw it as the unequivocal duty of the politicians and public servants to do as the Church bade them. In the words of Bishop Lucey, 'their position was that they were the final arbiters of right and wrong even in political matters'.[7] The public utterances of politician after politician in the Dáil debate on the Mother and Child scheme in 1951, as on other occasions, made it quite clear that most of them accepted this, and the same was true of most civil servants as well.

It was a feature of church-state contacts that they should be above all discreet and go unpublished. 'There was in fact a widespread feeling that it was somehow disedifying for the role of the Church to be examined in public.'[8] In the controversy over the mother and child scheme, one of the Taoiseach's charges against the Minister for Health, Noel Browne, was that he had gone public on it. John A. Costello took the view that:

> all this matter was intended to be private and to be adjusted behind closed doors and was never intended to be the subject of public controversy as it has been made by the former Minister for Health now.... All these matters could have been, and ought to have been, dealt with calmly in quiet and in council, without the public becoming aware of the matter. The public never ought to have become aware of the matter.[9]

As John Whyte commented, 'the fact that Mr Costello could unselfconsciously utter such words in 1951 is a sign of his confidence that Irish public opinion would generally agree with him.'[10]

The growing integration of church and state had its outward manifestations too. Politicians increasingly made a public profession of state deference to the Church. On taking up power in 1932, de Valera's government sent a message of 'respectful homage to the Pope': so, too, did his successor, John Costello, on behalf of the incoming inter-party government in 1948. In 1929, W. T. Cosgrave tried to hurry up the establishment of diplomatic relations with the Papacy to coincide with the centenary of Catholic Emancipation and, ironically, got into trouble with the Irish bishops whom he failed to consult. De Valera had no such difficulties when his government accorded the Eucharistic Congress of 1932 a state reception. It was at this time, too, that it became standard practice for public works, even very modest schemes, to be blessed on completion. At such ceremonies the attendance of representatives of both church and state was (and still is) *de rigueur* and there is no doubt who has precedence on such occasions. Aer Lingus, the state airline, had its fleet of aircraft publicly blessed on the tarmac at Dublin airport each year right up to the late sixties. The Censorship of Publications Board was during most of its existence chaired by a priest. Far from the public gaze, more shadowy organizations were at work to the same end. Some of the activities of a secret society like the Knights of Columbanus helped guide public policy decisions in the right direction, influenced administrative activities and perhaps had an impact on some public appointments.

As the Irish Catholic social movement got under way in the late thirties, there was a growing awareness of the need and potentialities for Catholics, both lay and clergy, to participate more vigorously in social activities and to propound Catholic solutions to social problems. An Irish Catholic sociology of a very conservative variety came into being developed by societies like the Christus Rex Society (founded in 1946) and others, and propagated in specifically Catholic papers and journals. Bodies like Muintir na Tíre (The Irish Community Development Movement), the Catholic Workers' College and others likewise contributed to the creation of a Catholic social order. One at least, Maria Duce, was 'more Papal than the Pope' and even embarrassed Irish bishops.

Commenting on the conservatism of the Irish clergy at this time, John Whyte pointed to a growing contrast between their approach and that of Catholics in some western European democracies in the years immediately after World War II:

> Irish Catholics continued to emphasize their distinctive traditions, at a time when continental Catholics were increasingly concerned to find common ground with those of other traditions, and in particular with democratic socialists. The result was that Irish Catholics were coming to look increasingly right-wing when compared with continental catholicism. [11]

Whyte noted that in following its traditional course, Irish catholicism was more like that in Portugal, Spain and Switzerland, all countries that had remained neutral during the war and escaped the post-war ferment.

Not surprisingly perhaps, there was sometimes an air of triumphalism in the attitudes and actions of Irish clergy in this period. In the twenties and thirties some issued instructions publicly on matters such as the licensing of dance halls. They also moved to prevent the appointment of a Protestant county librarian (and had the help of de Valera, then in opposition). In the forties, they were very ready, in Whyte's words, 'to give their flocks advice on how to apply Catholic principles in particular circumstances, even in matters where they had not hitherto been accustomed to speak.'[12] He cites the successful effort of the bishops of the Galway region to oust from her position as Mistress of Fox Hounds a Protestant lady who had been divorced and remarried. In 1948, the Archbishop of Armagh urged the Irish trade union movement to affiliate to the Federation of Christian Trade Unions and not the more socialist World Federation of Trade Unions. Bishops also flexed their muscles in the matter of Sunday opening hours. A pronouncement on this subject in 1950 stated unequivocally that even to argue for extended hours was a sin:

> Where there has been no existing and longstanding custom, to open public houses on Sundays even for a few hours would be a serious violation of this ecclesiastical law [Canon 1248]. So long as this ecclesiastical law remains it would be sinful to agitate for their opening. [13]

Where, as in matters to do with marriage, divorce etc., the position of Protestants was different from that of Catholics, Conor Cruise O'Brien was right to conclude that 'the State of the (95 per cent) Catholic nation can fairly be criticized for a certain insensitivity in relation to the rights and claims of the 5 per cent minority.'[14] The state, however, was doing nothing that Catholic people generally did not approve of. 'All the indications are that this degree of deference existed with the support of the people'.[15] The clergy whose precepts were being followed were not a pressure group of zealots beavering away in the context of public indifference: still less had they to stem a tide of liberal attitudes, as more recently, they have felt obliged to do.

In enshrining Catholic values in his Constitution, the devout de Valera was, as we have observed, only continuing the process of making the Irish state if not a confessional state, something closely akin to it. While he had been still in the wilderness in the early 1920s, the Cumann na nGaedheal government had demonstrated in its legislation what Whyte describes as 'the puritan streak in Irish Catholicism' with the Censorship of Films Act, 1923 and the Intoxicating Liquor Act, 1927. Later, it followed with the Censorship of Publications Act, 1929, under which publications could be banned if they were 'indecent or obscene' or if they advocated the unnatural prevention of conception or the procurement of abortion or miscarriage. Early on, the same government also snuffed out the private bill procedure (in the Oireachtas) by which a divorce might be obtained, a carry-over from the days of British rule. When Fianna Fáil assumed power in 1932, it 'proved as willing as it s predecessors to employ the powers of the state in safeguarding moral standards.'[16] Section 17 of the Criminal Law Amendment Act, 1935, prohibited the sale and importation of contraceptives and in the same year the Public Dance Halls Act laid down a new system for controlling public dances, a constant obsession of the Irish clergy.

Although *Bunreacht na hEireann* was not occasioned by the need to make Irish fundamental law more Catholic, its preparation presented the opportunity to do so and most commentators have called it a Catholic Constitution. However, as our discussion of it in chapter three suggests, it is better to view it as de Valera's effort to grapple with the fundamental problems that faced him and to bring and hold together the two traditions that were reflected in Ireland. The attempt to conflate the principles from both traditions is very obvious in the rights articles, the section to which most writers refer when they speak of the Catholic nature of the Constitution. 'Certain of the fundamental rights are couched in language of a secular nationalist nature while others are clearly and strongly inspired by the Christian view of natural law'.[17] Elsewhere, although the very first words of the Preamble, signal the Christian and, more specifically, Catholic nature of the document, it was not markedly Catholic. Only in Article 15 (functional or vocational councils) and in Articles 18 and 19 (on Seanad Eireann) was there a specifically Catholic provision. Some articles, on the contrary, fell short of satisfying contemporary Catholic teaching, notably Article 44 where, as we have noted, de Valera experienced his biggest difficulties.

Once enacted, *Bunreacht na hEireann* tended to be viewed by de Valera and Fianna Fáil in particular, but also the country in general, as a finished product. It was, as we have already dubbed it, a 'normative' constitution. Consequently, there was little disposition to amend it, particularly in this period when the basic attitudes and values of the community continued largely unchanged. Nor was there much constitutional development of any kind. The disposition of the politicians to accept the conservative, anti-state teaching of Irish Catholic sociology and to view the rights articles as an appropriate mix for Irish people meant that there would be no initiatives from that direction. This was the situation for thirty years or so from its enactment.

Even initiatives by churchmen themselves got nowhere. Both the belated attempt to apply vocational principles seen in the Commission on Vocational Organization (1943), which was chaired by the Bishop of Galway, and the proposal in 1944 for a revised national health insurance scheme made by the Bishop of Clonfert, the state-appointed chairman of the National Health Insurance Society, came to nothing. They were brushed off by Fianna Fáil governments probably egged on quietly by senior civil servants. Whyte sees these rebuffs to churchmen as heralding the beginning of a period of strain between church and state, but the bishops generally chose not to make an issue of them.

Where they did so choose, a few years later, it was a different story. The issue was the reform of health services and in particular the provision of maternity and child welfare services. The story of Dr Noel Browne's 'mother and child' scheme in 1951 has become part of Irish political folklore. What is often overlooked is that its Fianna Fáil-inspired predecessor, the Health Act, 1947, had also evoked a protest from the Hierarchy, and its successor, the Health Bill, 1953, was only rescued by a quiet intervention and salvage operation by de Valera himself. This involved some judicious amendments to make it acceptable to the Hierarchy whose objections extended beyond possible dangers for Catholic mothers to matters that revealed a marked degree of anti-state bias. These included universal provision without a means test, the funding of medical schools by local authorities, and a percieved threat to the voluntary hospitals many of which were controlled, and some owned, by religious orders.

Although the circumstances made constitutional amendment unlikely in any area in which the Church had an interest — or in any other area either — there was one attempt to mount a pressure-group campaign by a Catholic 'fringe' organization. Among the Catholic sociologists, publicists and active members of social movements there were a few whose application of Catholic principles as they understood them was extreme and even embarrassing to the orthodox. In the late 1940s, one such, Maria Duce, began to campaign for an amendment of the 'special position' provision in Article 44 to provide for the recognition of the church as, in the words of its programme, 'the One True Church' which is 'divinely appointed to teach man what favours or hinders his supernatural destiny'. This would have destroyed the compromise formula so carefully devised by de Valera and generally, if in some quarters reluctantly, accepted by the Irish bishops. Although it got the support of one county council, perhaps without that body realising what it was doing, it was not endorsed by the major parties or leading politicians. Some of them no doubt were waiting for a signal from the bishops: it never came. Although what Maria Duce sought was essentially a Catholic position as put forward in the first draft of Article 44 (see above p. 28), the organization generally smacked of zealotry, and it got no overt support from the bishops, and in particular the influential Archbishop of Dublin. Nevertheless, extreme as Maria Duce now appears to have been, it attracted support numbered in thousands.

It was, rather, by judicial interpretation that the Catholicization of the law proceeded. Though not without some qualification, *Bunreacht na hEireann* was generally seen as a Catholic Constitution, the 'coping stone' of a sustained movement to Catholicize the law and government. In interpreting those of its provisions which dealt with the rights and duties of individuals and the state, the undoubted intentions of its authors would be relevant and, given the Catholic origins of some articles, it would be reasonable to have regard to the abiding principles behind their wording, in particular the precepts of natural law. Some leading legal authorities began to turn in this direction. The natural law, one said, ought to be 'the sheet anchor' of the Constitution: another saw the Constitution as 'accepting the Thomistic philosophy of the natural law'.[18]

This line of thought had some influence on Irish jurisprudence. In the circumstances what is noteworthy is not how much, but how little. However, this is easily explained. Irish lawyers of the time were steeped in the British tradition of the Common Law and judicial precedent and, naturally, the judges, senior members of a notoriously conservative profession, were slow, even reluctant, to grasp the opportunity opened up for creative interpretation offered by the existence of the new Constitution which specifically gave them the power to review. Or rather, most judges were. One, however, Mr Justice Gavan Duffy, was a notable exception, and he, as it happened, was strongly republican, a supporter of de Valera and imbued with what one of his successors, Mr Justice Kenny, described as 'very militant Catholicism.'[19]

Already a judge of the High Court when the Constitution was enacted and its president from 1946-51, 'he was one of the most important judicial innovators that Ireland has had.'[20] Natural law, as Catholics defined and understood it, had hitherto hardly made an appearance in the judgements of the Irish courts. In one case, in 1935, Chief Justice Kennedy had given it as his opinion in a dissenting judgement that if any legislation 'were repugnant to the Natural Law, such legislation would be necessarily unconstitutional and invalid.'[21] Following him, Gavan Duffy, in a sustained effort to deny the validity of English precedents and to replace them with decisions based on Catholic principles, showed what potential there was for invoking natural law, establishing a set of Catholic rights and, generally, for Catholicizing Irish law. In doing so, he made painfully clear what this might mean for the rights of Protestants.

Beginning in the early forties, 'in a series of innovatory judgements' Gavan Duffy 'sought to clarify the juridical status of the Catholic church'.[22] In 1943 in the *Maguire* case he departed from the precedents governing charities (which required them to be for public benefit) to hold that a gift for a contemplative order for the perpetual adoration of the Blessed Sacrament was a charity, saying in his judgement, 'it is a shock to one's sense of propriety, and a grave discredit to the law that there should in this Catholic country be any doubt about the validity of such a bequest.'[23] In *Cook* v. *Carroll*, a seduction case, he upheld a priest's refusal to divulge to the court what the girl involved had told him, basing his decision not to follow British precedents explicitly on the 'special position' of the Catholic church in the Constitution:

> In a state where nine out of every ten citizens today are Catholic and on a matter closely touching the religious outlook of the people, it would be intolerable that the common law, as expounded after the Reformation in a Protestant land, should be taken to bind a nation which persistently repudiated the Reformation as heresy.... I hold that the emergence of the national Constitution is a complete and conclusive answer to the objection that I have no judicial precedent in favour of the parish priest.[24]

In the *Tilson* case which raised the question of the validity of a pre-nuptial agreement made by the parents in a mixed marriage to bring up any children as Catholics, Gavan Duffy was dealing with a sensitive issue of human rights that perhaps more than any other aroused Protestant anger and apprehension. He departed from the existing Common Law rule that a father was entitled to determine the religion of his children and the previous refusal of the courts to recognize the binding character of such pre-marriage agreements. In doing so, he declared that:

> an order of the Court designed to secure the fulfillment of an agreement, peremptorily required before a "mixed marriage" by the Church whose special position in Ireland is officially recognized as the guardian of the faith of the Catholic spouse cannot be witheld on any grounds of public policy by the very state which pays homage to that Church.[25]

However, on appeal, the Supreme Court in effect ignored this line of argument, though for different reasons they came to the same conclusion. Later, in 1964, the Guardianship of Infants Act gave statutory effect to the principle that the welfare of the child is paramount.

In these cases as elsewhere, Judge Gavan Duffy was to a great extent a lone voice, though at one point Mr Justice Lavery appeared to be heading down the same road. In 1945, in a bigamy case where the ecclesiastical authorities in effect chose to regard as invalid a registry office marriage between a Catholic and a Protestant and knowingly sanctioned a second marriage, he imposed a trivial penalty. Holding that it 'could not be regarded as a flagrant type of case', he quoted Articles 42 and 44 of the Constitution.[26] Generally, however, their fellow judges did not follow these leads. Gavan Duffy in particular is important rather because his judgements showed clearly where a thoroughly Catholic approach to the Constitution could have taken Irish law. The implications of developing his line of reasoning for the tiny non-Catholic minority inside the state and for the chances of wooing Northern Unionists into an all-Ireland republic, which was the ambition of de Valera and most other Irish people, are obvious.

Perhaps there never was much danger of the courts developing the Constitution along these lines. In this period few cases involving constitutional issues came before the courts and, as we have observed, the judges felt considerable inhibitions when it came to interpreting the Constitution. Consequently, as McWhinney concluded in his *Judicial Review in the English-Speaking World*, up to the middle sixties at least 'the impact of modern Catholic political, social, and economic ideas on legal development was rather less significant or substantial than the adoption of the radically new Constitution of 1937 might have seemed at the time to foreshadow.'[27] Nevertheless, Gavan Duffy was right: 1937 *was* a new departure. By the time more adventurous judges were at work, times were changing and with them the intellectual climate, in some quarters at least. The potential for development that Chief Justice O Dálaigh and some of his colleagues were to discern and exploit would be markedly different from what Gavan Duffy saw. In some respects, as we shall see, the direction they would seem to be taking would alarm the Church.[28]

— 5 —

The Church and Constitutional Change

FROM THE EARLY nineteen-sixties Irish society began to change quite quickly. The Republic experienced substantial industrialization, a period of rapid economic growth and considerable demographic changes. Although it was still in the late eighties a rural and agricultural country by Western European standards, the proportion of the population living in rural areas had declined at a faster rate than hitherto and by 1980 had fallen to less than half; the number employed in agriculture had also decreased rapidly and by 1980 had fallen below twenty per cent; and the age structure of the population had also altered so that by the late seventies half was under twenty-five years.

Growing affluence was enhanced by the sudden big rise in agricultural incomes consequent upon accession to the European Economic Community and the benefits of the Common Agricultural Policy (CAP). Membership of the European Communities also had the more general effect of widening the horizons of Irish people, though it was undoubtedly access to television that did most to bring about this change. In short, the country became, belatedly, a typical post-World War II affluent society with more and more people enjoying the life styles of the peoples of the richest western countries.

These changes were precisely of the kind that, as David Martin has observed, are conducive to 'secularization' in a society.[1] Secularization is 'that process by which many sections of society and culture are removed from the influence of religious values, institutions and symbols.'[2] As a society becomes secularized, the roles of religion and of the Church are attenuated. The Church no longer pervades all life. Much economic and political activity and, in time, more and more aspects of social life come to be regarded as separate from religion. There is also a decline in religious practice and a growing tendency for individuals to decide for themselves what is right and wrong perhaps, but not necessarily, taking account of the precepts of their Church. Instead, 'Christianity and its professional guardians are partly winkled out of the structure of legitimation and become more marginal to local and national élites. The clergy . . . presides over [a] voluntary association.'[3]

Some sections of Irish society were displaying such secularist attitudes in the nineteen-sixties, but the pace and extent of change are hard to measure and often overstated. They were most obvious in those areas of social activity where middle-class intellectuals tended to take the lead, such as broadcasting and journalism, and among young people. Significantly, in the early seventies the church itself began to monitor the practice of religion as measured by attendance at mass and the extent of religious belief. By that time there were some signs of falling away among city people and the young, and attitudes to sex, divorce, homosexuality and drugs confirmed this. A decade later the trend was more pronounced, more and more younger people indicating a weaker acceptance of orthodox beliefs and of the authority of the Church.[4]

The extent of these changes was nevertheless modest. What astonished most foreigners was rather the persistence of high levels of belief and practice among Irish people. In 1985, 87 per cent of people of eighteen years and over attended mass weekly: in 1974 the figure had been 91 per cent. In 1985 also, over 70 per cent accepted Papal infallibility as compared with over 80 per cent a decade earlier. A community with patterns of habits and beliefs such as these is a long way from being a secular society, and although people's attitudes to issues such as contraception and divorce were undoubtedly becoming more permissive, the rate of change was slow and it was not until about 1980 that opinion polls began to report a majority favouring the legalization of divorce in some circumstances. Moreover, the reformers of the seventies discovered that when they raised the issue of contraception formally by proposing legislation, public opinion, alerted by Catholic pressure groups and exhorted by the clergy, hardened temporarily against them as the opinion polls showed. Their experience was only a foretaste of what was to come in the middle eighties.

The threat to the Church's hold arising from modernization was increased at this time by the pressures due to the exacerbation of the Northern Ireland situation from the late sixties. In his time, de Valera had come up against the incompatibility of traditional nationalist aspirations: when Northern Ireland erupted into continuous civil disobedience and sporadic guerilla warfare from 1968 onwards, church leaders had willy-nilly to face the same problem. By this time it had begun to dawn on significant numbers in the Republic that there were two communities on the island of Ireland, each with its own tradition and culture and each with legitimate aspirations that had to be accommodated. As more and more came to accept this, demands were generated for constitutional and legislative changes that, it was hoped, would make union of some sort with the Republic more acceptable to Northern Protestants. If there was to be any hope at all of a peaceful solution, Irish society had to become more pluralist, but some of the proposed reforms raised moral issues on which the Churches in Ireland disagreed. Thus, Catholic Church leaders, especially the more nationalist of them, confronted a cruel dilemma. The Church which had in the past supported and even identified with the nationalist movement might now be seen as thwarting nationalist aspirations were it to insist on retaining Catholic standards and practices.

The changes which the reformers who were both nationalist and pluralist, thought the government of the Republic ought to make were clearly spelled out by the early nineteen-seventies, notably by Garret FitzGerald in *Towards a New Ireland* (1972). Among them were matters of great concern to the Catholic Church, including the proposal to remove the 'special position' clause and the bar on divorce legislation, both in the Constitution; the amendment of the law banning the import and sale of contraceptives; and changes in the censorship laws. Increasingly, such reforms came to be advocated as in any case desirable in a twenty-six county context in order to do justice to the small non-Catholic minority and to create a pluralist society as a desirable end in itself.

II

If a theocratic state is, as Tom Inglis defined it, 'one in which the state is unwilling or unable to enact a law which is contrary to the moral law defined by the Church',[5] the Irish state might justly have been called 'theocratic' during its first forty years. The demands arising from modernization and the exigencies of the Northern Ireland situation put increasing strain on this pattern of relationships. In the words of Liam Ryan, 'the years from 1960 ... can best be described in sociological language as years of "tension management", tension between the old and the new: ... between the ways of God and the ways of the world.'[6]

Before we consider this development, however, it is necessary to notice the changes in the Church itself. It must not be assumed that any change in the stance of the Church in Ireland or any shift in the pattern of church-state relationships was forced upon an entirely conservative and unchanging Hierarchy. Modernization affected the Roman Catholic Church as an institution as it did the rest of western society. Although the Church in Ireland and Irish Catholics generally had not been as much influenced by the modernizing changes that occurred in Catholic thought and practice as those in some other European countries after the second world war, they could not but be affected by the process of *aggiornamento* which got under way in the Roman Catholic Church as a whole in and after the pontificate of John XXIII and the Second Vatican Council (1962–65). In particular the marked shift towards accepting pluralism and promoting ecumenism was to have enormous repercussions. That the Church was no longer seeking special recognition or special privileges from the state was of particular relevance to Ireland: so were the intervenionist statements in the Encyclical *Mater et Magistra* (1961): so, too, was the encouragement of discussion and debate on controversial matters and the added stress on individual conscience.

Although the reaction of some Irish bishops to the changing climate was cautious to say the least, subjects like marriage, divorce, contraception, the relationships between the clergy and the laity, the role of the state and church-state relations were now, whether they liked it or not, coming under discussion, sometimes very public discussion in the media. Some urban, middle-class Catholics in particular were quick to reject the rules and relationships that the

Irish clergy had traditionally operated and that had been well enough suited to a rural peasant people. As it happened, there were enough of a new generation of Irish bishops to come to terms with the inevitable challenges to traditional teaching and practices. Among them were men sensitive to what was going on in continental western Europe where the Church had willy-nilly to coexist with other religions, to learn to live with the affluent society and to recognize its own limited ability to affect political behaviour in pluralist societies.

Because of these differences between the conservative and the modern wing of the Hierarchy, that body's public pronouncements were occasionally equivocal and individual bishops sometimes expressed views that seemed to differ from those of their colleagues. In spite of these equivocations and differences, the main lines of change and the limits of permissible change were clear. First, there was a move away from the 'integralist' position that had been so markedly developed up to the fifties: second, in respect of the law on matters that raised questions of sexual morality and the sacredness of human life, the line was to be held. Both had important consequences for constitutional development.

III

The 'special position' provision in Article 44 of *Bunreacht na hEireann*, one of the items in de Valera's 'odd bouquet' for Northern Protestants, was an obvious target for those who advocated a pluralist society. In 1967, the Committee on the Constitution, one of Sean Lemass's instruments of political modernization, recommended the deletion of the offending clauses. These clauses, the committee reported, 'give offence to non-Catholics and are also a useful weapon in the hands of those who are anxious to emphasise the difference between North and South.' Significantly, they noted that it was clearly to be inferred from decisions taken in the Second Vatican Council 'that the Catholic Church does not seek any special recognition or privilege as compared with other religions.'[7]

For politicians to point this out was a sign that a wind of change was beginning to blow in Dublin, if only as yet gently. In political circles, hitherto, great care had been taken to make sure that such topics did not appear on the political agenda. Here now was an all-party committee deliberately raising an apparently contentious issue and interpreting Vatican documents for themselves. That committee's report was hastily buried, but their interpretation was right, and in 1969 Cardinal Conway cleared the path for amendment. A Northern Ireland man, he chose to do so in that context:

> I personally would not shed a single tear if the relevant sub-sections of Article 44 were to disappear. It confers no legal privilege whatever on the Catholic Church and, if the way to convince our fellow Christians in the North about this is to remove it, then it might be worth the expense of a referendum.[9]

When, in 1972, the Fifth Amendment of the Constitution Bill providing for the deletion of sections 2 and 3 of Article 44.1 was being debated in the Dáil, politicians of all parties fell over one another to support the change and some went so far as to condemn the inclusion of the offending sections in the first place. There was even a disposition to go further and urge the need for an entirely new Constitution 'without all this effusive, ecclesiastical moralising of the present Constitution of the Republic.'[10] The sense of the debate was clear: the Church had given a green light and this measure was to be a first instalment of constitutional change.

To make the Constitution more acceptable to Northern Protestants was however a hazardous undertaking. The Hierarchy soon made it clear that for the time being 'enough is enough', as we shall see. What this burst of initiative did do though was to raise the broad issue of the extent of the state's duty to follow Catholic teaching and advice as tendered by the bishops and to evoke a new definition of church-state relations. It arose in 1973 in the context of the introduction by three Senators of a bill to permit the importation and sale of contraceptives. A statement by the Hierarchy strongly condemning any relaxation of the law included what amounted to a redefinition of the Church's view of the state's obligations to the Church:

> There are many things which the Catholic church holds to be morally wrong and no one has ever suggested, least of all the Church herself, that they should be prohibited by the State.... What the legislators have to decide is whether a change in the law would, on balance, do more harm than

> good, by damaging the character of the society for which they
> are responsible. ... We emphasise that it is not a matter for
> the bishops to decide whether the law should be changed or
> not. That is a matter for the legislators, after a conscientious
> consideration of all the factors involved.[11]

This new stance, which was clearly in line with post-Vatican II
policy, was reiterated on a number of occasions, notably to the
New Ireland Forum in 1984 by Bishop Cahal Daly on behalf of
the Hierarchy. Speaking about the position of the Church on
'questions of public morality' he said:

> We have repeatedly declared that we in no way seek to have
> the moral teaching of the Catholic church become the criterion
> of constitutional change or to have the principles of Catholic
> faith enshrined in civil law.[12]

On the face of it, the bishops seemed to be claiming that, when
it comes to public policy making, the Church is a pressure group
seeking to have its views taken into consideration along with other
points of view and interests by those whose job it is to make the
decisions. The 1973 statement was explicit on this but — and it
is a big but — as John Whyte put it, 'the analogy between the
hierarchy and other interest groups breaks down because in a mainly
Catholic country, the Catholic hierarchy has a weapon which no
other interest group possesses: its authority over men's consciences.'[13]
He is right for, as Bishop Daly put it:

> What we have claimed, and what we must claim, is the right
> to fulfil our pastoral duty ... to alert the consciences of
> Catholics to the moral consequences of any proposed piece
> of legislation and to the impact of that legislation on the moral
> quality of life in society.[14]

In practice, although the Church in principle now accorded more
autonomy to the individual conscience, Irish clergy continued to
make it abundantly clear to politicians where Catholic duty lay
in terms suggesting that they did not view the church as just another
pressure group. One of the more conservative put it thus: 'Politicians
who profess to be Catholics are not entitled to follow their
consciences in a void, as if a teaching authority did not exist in
the Catholic Church.'[15] He went further: 'The Catholic people of
our state have a right — a political right — to have the provision
of the kind of social framework that supports them in the living

out of their moral and religious principles.'[16] What is more, when circumstances seemed to demand it, the clergy could and would mobilize the electorate to exercise their democratic right to have the last say, provided they said the right thing. Some politicians might deplore it, but in the Ireland of the seventies and eighties the bulk of the faithful would still take advice or directions — when does the one become the other? — from their clergy on matters which they saw as falling within their domain.

IV

From the early seventies, questions of rights involving proposals to amend the Constitution or alter statutes constantly figured on the political agenda. Some of them raised issues of sexual morality or the family and were thus of considerable concern to the Church. It was in the context of one of these, contraception, that the 1973 principle was enunciated; and of two others, abortion and divorce, that that principle fell to be applied, though not without some fudging and obvious signs of disagreement among the bishops. These were not the only rights issues to arise, but in matters such as adoption in 1974 and the provision of multi-denominational schools later in the decade the bishops took less rigid lines than their predecessors and agreement was come to between church and state comparatively easily. Contraception, abortion and divorce were different matters altogether.

During the seventies, Church leaders in Ireland became alarmed by the trends in western society generally and dismayed at the evident pattern of judicial decisions in rights cases. They anticipated and feared the domino effect of softening on moral issues. In Rome, too, there were increasing signs of a hardening of opinion. It is against this background that these issues were confronted in Ireland.

Contraception was a contentious matter throughout the seventies. In the early years of the decade, attempts were made by backbenchers to get it aired by introducing bills relaxing the prohibition on the import and sale of contraceptives. These were condemned by the Church and viewed with disfavour by most party leaders who, as always, preferred not to have the subject raised. But raised it was, by the judgement of the Supreme Court in the *McGee* case (*McGee* v. *Attorney General* [1974] IR 284) which by finding the relevant section of the Criminal Law Amendment Act, 1935, to be unconstitutional because it violated Mrs. McGee's rights, opened the door to the importation of contraceptives and pointed to the possibility of the courts legalizing their sale in the future. With this and the increasing acceptability and use of contraceptives, the law obviously had to be revised. Successive governments agonized over the subject and eventually in 1979 Charles Haughey, then Minister for Health, grasped the nettle and introduced a restrictive measure that provided for the sale of contraceptives on prescription for adequate medical reasons. This measure, Haughey's 'Irish solution to an Irish problem',[17] unworkable as it so patently was, was superseded in 1985 after a considerable political struggle by the Family Planning (Amendment) Act which legalized the sale of contraceptives to anyone over eighteen.

The passage of this measure, pushed through with great vigour and perseverence by Barry Desmond, then Minister for Health:

> marked a landmark in two ways. First, it was, with the exception of the Licensing Act 1960, the only bill to be passed through the Oireachtas against the advice of a number of bishops. Second, and more important, it was, if reports in the media are to be believed, the first bill in an area where the hierarchy have a traditional interest to be introduced and passed without consultation with the hierarchy. [18]

Not without reason, it was seen as the triumph of pluralist politicians over the Church. Although the hostility of the Church was made very clear, the official stance of the Hierarchy conformed to the 1973 principle: it was for the clergy to give guidance to Catholics and for the politicians to decide. However, some bishops and many other clergy did not adhere to that line, and by adopting a harder and more traditional stance heightened the impression of a confrontation between the Church and the state which the Church lost. In the case of the other two issues, where referendums, i.e. the people as a whole, were involved, it was a very different story.

V

By the late seventies, Church leaders and conservative opinion generally were alarmed at the direction and speed of the tide of public opinion in sex and family matters. More specifically, they feared the tendency of the courts to identify new constitutional rights as the judges developed the doctrine of unspecified human rights. Under the Offences against the Person Act, 1861, abortion was illegal in Ireland, but was it not possible, in view of what was going on elsewhere in the western world, that a rights case taken in a set of deserving circumstances might evoke a favourable decision? Might not then the door be open? Perhaps not immediately, but in time, there might be proposals for legislation to permit abortion in certain circumstances as was the position elsewhere. The campaign for the insertion of an article into the Constitution forbidding abortion was a deliberate attempt by conservative Catholics to head off both the courts and the Oireachtas. In April 1981, a number of Catholic organizations pursuing this aim came together to form an umbrella organization, the Pro-Life Amendment Campaign (PLAC). A powerful pressure group campaign was mounted, organised and directed by skilled practitioners, backed with American money and, so it seemed, American 'know-how'.

The political circumstances were unusually propitious for pressure groups. In a period of eighteen months in 1981-82 there were three general elections. The political scales were evenly balanced and this situation presented unrivalled opportunities to extract promises from party leaders. Both FitzGerald and Haughey were asked for, and gave, undertakings to introduce legislation and mount a referendum. Although at first it appeared that Fine Gael, Fianna Fáil and Church leaders who were consulted were agreed on a suitable form of words, the coalition government's decision to introduce a different formula because of legal doubts about the first one being workable broke the consensus. The bishops decided in favour of the original (Fianna Fáil) wording but Protestant Church leaders sided with the Government. Amid accusations of sectarianism, secularisation and bad faith, the government wording was defeated in Dáil Eireann and the original put to referendum.

By now, it was evident that political war of an unprecedented kind had broken out on a sensitive and divisive issue. Without doubt, this was the last thing the Hierarchy desired. They had not been involved in the setting up or subsequent activities of PLAC, though their statement of March 1983 supported the proposal for an amendment as 'prudent anticipation'.[19] When rival clauses were being canvassed, they came out against the Government's, but all along their official position was that of the 1973 declaration. Their statement of 22 August 1983, though it advised Catholics that the proposed amendment would safeguard the rights of both mother and unborn child and recalled the words of the Pope on his visit to Limerick a short time previously, specifically recognized the right of every person to vote according to his or her conscience.

Many priests and some bishops were by no means so meticulous about following the 1973 principle. Dr Gaetano Alibrandi, the Papal Nuncio, at a mass in Kerry recalled the defeat of the Turks by the Christians at the battle of Lepanto in 1571 and assured his listeners that on referendum day, 'the world will be watching Ireland'[20]. Thus encouraged, many clergy threw themselves into what they did indeed see as a battle for the faith against the spread of secular values. As John Cooney observed, 'throughout the land the pulpits of the Catholic Churches thundered with the simplistic message to the faithful that to vote against the amendment would be to vote for abortion.'[21] The amendment was duly passed.

What was inserted into the Constitution by the Eighth Amendment of the Constitution Act, 1983, was an addition to Article 40, the personal rights article:

> The State acknowledges the right to life of the unborn and, with due regard to the equal right to life of the mother, guarantees in its laws to respect, and, as far as practicable, by its laws to defend and vindicate that right.

To the clergy and a large number of Catholics a human rights clause is exactly what it was: to others, and particularly the leaders of the Protestant churches and many of their congregations, it was a needless, sectarian addition. Both they and those who followed Garret FitzGerald in his efforts to make the society more pluralist felt that they had suffered a setback. They were quickly to suffer another, but this time they brought it upon themselves.

VI

The reform of the marriage laws, now obviously incapable of coping with the problem of breakdown, and particularly the prohibition in the Constitution on a divorce law was an integral part of Garret FitzGerald's constitutional crusade. This ban was regarded by Northern Protestants as the very symbol of 'Rome rule', almost

as offensive to them as Articles 2 and 3. Both for this reason —
that at the very least it was necessary to deprive Northern Protestants
of a debating point and at most that it might remove an obstacle
to a possible political union of North and South — and out of
a genuine desire to move towards a more pluralist state, FitzGerald
and those who thought like him desired to have the Constitution
amended. By the early eighties the opinion polls seemed to suggest
that a majority might now favour a law allowing divorce in some
circumstances.

The victory in November 1982 of a Fine Gael and Labour
Party coalition dominated by FitzGerald and those who thought
like him and had for some years been in favour of removing the
ban, seemed to offer an opportunity to tackle the issue. The manifesto
of the incoming coalition, *Programme for Government*, promised
an Oireachtas committee to consider problems of marriage
breakdown and to report within a year. However, the abortion issue
intervened and the controversy it evoked dragged on, making many
politicians loath to tackle any issues of this kind. It was not until
April 1985 that the committee reported. It produced valuable
recommendations on a number of aspects of marriage failure but
its members were divided on divorce and, although they ended by
recommending a referendum, they failed to produce a proposal for
the kind of divorce law that should be enacted once the ban was
removed.

By this time, the pressure group campaigns both for and against
were well under way, not least that of the Hierarchy. The bishops
were smarting at the lack of consultation on the contraception bill
which had been rammed through the Oireachtas by a determined
minister backed by a majority in the cabinet. Also they were very
conscious after the abortion referendum experience of what could
be achieved by mobilizing the public. A pastoral letter, *Love is
for Life*, had already been read out in all Catholic churches on
three successive Sundays in March. It declared that 'no legislative
enactment can dissolve a valid marriage and leave the partner free
to marry again. Remarriage of a civilly divorced person is not a
real marriage in the sight of God.'[22] After considerable government
hesitation and delay, the Oireachtas committee report was eventually
discussed in the Dáil in a debate notable for the strange reluctance
to contribute on the part of usually voluble members now clearly

fearing, in the words of one of them, to find themselves 'within the radiation zone of possible episcopal wrath.'[23]

The parliamentary process completed, FitzGerald consulted the leaders of all religions, seeking their views on a number of areas of marriage law. By this time the situation was thoroughly unsatisfactory. A long confusing debate in the media conducted by the pressure groups on each side was agitating and confusing the public; parties were divided; and the various churches found themselves on opposite sides of a sectarian divide. The consultations only confirmed what was well known, that on the key issue, divorce, non-Catholic Churches favoured the removal of the absolute ban and the Catholic Church took the view that 'even a limited form of divorce law ... would be harmful to society.'[24] On the question of whether to hold a referendum, the 1973 principle was applied on both sides. According to Cardinal Ó Fiaich, the Taoiseach did not ask the bishops and they in turn did not proffer any advice. That was, he said, an entirely political decision: 'the Taoiseach will have to make up his mind.'[25]

With the opinion polls still indicating a slowly growing majority in favour of allowing divorce in some circumstances and with impetus added by the success of the Anglo-Irish Agreement giving rise to hopes of movement on that front, FitzGerald decided to go forward. Committed as he was, he recognized that if he did not do so at that point, as the Government's term of office was coming to an end, he might justly be charged with reneging on his undertaking. He and his colleagues recognized that the political situation was far from favourable, with inter-party differences in the coalition and intra-party differences inside Fine Gael. Fianna Fáil, though officially taking no stand, would unofficially campaign against the removal. The experience over abortion showed what a Catholic campaign could achieve and some of FitzGerald's party colleagues believed that the Government and the party were courting disaster.

So they were: the subsequent events were a repeat of 1983. Catholic clergy with varying degrees of circumspection advised their congregations to vote against the removal of the ban, some on the grounds that that was the Church's teaching; others on the wider grounds that society as a whole would be harmed. Some stressed the rights of individuals to follow their consciences, others did not. Some agonized over the right of minorities, others did not, among them Bishop Newman:

> The fact that other Christian Churches have allowed it must
> not weigh with us Catholics. The fact that a few of our own
> priests and theologians would seem to favour it must not weigh
> with us either. There are always people like that, but we must
> stand by the faith.[26]

The lay partisans on both sides were outspoken, but the anti-divorce
faction was greatly superior in resources, organization and tactics.
The terms of the Government's proposed restrictive divorce
legislation, should the amendment be passed, did not sink in. In
the public mind the issue was perceived simply as divorce or no
divorce. Arguments adduced to alarm voters and particularly women
voters were bandied about with great abandon. Those warning of
possible dangers to family and succession rights and particularly
to the position of wives and children of the first family were said
by some commentators to have had a decisive impact on the result.
On the contrary, as others have pointed out, analysis of the vote
shows a pattern very similar to that at the abortion referendum
in 1983. Michael Gallagher put it as follows:

> The no vote ... (63.5 per cent) was very close nationally to
> the 1983 Yes vote (66.9 per cent) and, moreover, the patterns
> on a constituency by constituency basis are practically identical.
> ... In 1986, all bar one constituency voted just as in
> 1983, ...[27]

He concluded that 'the common theme is obviously the place of
Catholic values in Irish society.'[28]

When it came to 'Catholic values' the majority in the Republic
in the middle eighties evidently continued to pay heed to the
exhortations of their clergy. The conclusion from data collected
for Market Research Bureau of Ireland surveys in 1983 and 1987
was that 'home and Church are seen as the main sources of influence
on marriage and family life; the Church itself followed by the home,
are most influential on divorce and abortion.'[29] There can be little
doubt of that. As referendum day approached and the electorate
really faced the issues, the critical swing in opinion showed
dramatically what was the political reality. (See diagram opposite.)

Clearly, the operation of the 1973 principle gave to bishops
exercising their democratic right to lobby politicians and exhort
the electorate, the ability to influence decisively political outcomes

in matters which they regarded as vital to Church interests. The 1973 principle was enunciated in good faith and some bishops applied it circumspectly, but it was inoperable because some of their number and some, perhaps many, of the clergy could and did talk in more traditional terms and were listened to with traditional respect and obedience. They did not believe that politicians had the right to make up their own minds on some matters and they made that clear. They had active, if sometimes embarrassing, lay allies in the Catholic organizations that showed their muscle in these two campaigns. Thus, the bishops could, for the time being, have it both ways.

What these experiences also showed was that the Church would seek to impose the basic values of the majority and would not concede a claim as of right to something that the bishops themselves did not — and could not — concede as being right. It would not therefore contribute to the creation of a pluralist society in the Republic or even, if the question were seriously to arise, in an all-Ireland state. The erosion of its position and role in society and its ability to influence people is almost certainly inevitable but it will be slow.

Attitudes to Divorce Issue

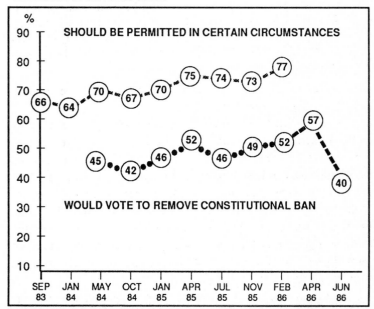

Source: MRBI *Irish Times Survey,* June 1986, published in *The Irish Times,* 25 June 1986.

—— 6 ——

The Courts and the Constitution

THE CENTRAL ARGUMENT of this book is that the constitution of a democratic country ought to be 'normative', i.e. it should be an actual political force, respected and obeyed because it reflects the traditions, culture and standards of the people. To that end, it must be capable of being constantly adjusted, and perhaps occasionally recast, to reflect alterations in political practice and changes in community values. It needs to be in process of continual development. Those who devise constitutions usually provide for this by including in them arrangements for changing them in the form of a procedure for amending the text. It should not be thought, however, that constitutions can be changed only by amendment. Courts of law also can acquire the role of constitutional developers where, as is often the case, they have the legal power to review, that is 'to invalidate on constitutional grounds any act of any government agency — legislative, executive, administrative, police or judicial'.[1]

The superior courts in the Irish system, the High Court and the Supreme Court, have such powers. These are either stated in *Bunreacht na hEireann* or have been inferred by the courts themselves. The power to review legislation is explicitly stated. Article $15.4.1^0$ forbids the Oireachtas from enacting any law repugnant to the Constitution and, in Article $34.3.2^0$, the jurisdiction of the High Court is stated as extending 'to the question of the validity of any law having regard to the provisions of the Constitution'. Under Article $34.4.3^0$, such questions may go on appeal to the Supreme Court. In addition, the Supreme Court has the duty to consider any bill referred to it by the President of Ireland under Article 26 to establish 'whether such Bill or any specified provision or provisions of such Bill is or are repugnant to this Constitution or to any provision thereof.' Besides questions concerning legislation, the High Court and the Supreme Court consider cases where public authorities and individuals or groups are in dispute over alleged violations of constitutional rights and where questions arise about the proper spheres of action of organs of government.

The powers of the High Court and the Supreme Court to invalidate laws are not absolute. The constitutions of most states — and Ireland is one of these — contain dispensing provisions for emergencies which enable the government to by-pass the usual constitutional restrictions and to pass laws that cannot be challenged in the courts. If, in Ireland, in a time of war or armed rebellion as defined in Article 28.3.3^0 of the Constitution, the Oireachtas has resolved that a 'national emergency' exists, no law 'expressed to be for the purpose of securing the public safety and the preservation of the state' can be invalidated. Whether the reservations about this provision expressed by the Supreme Court in a case in 1976 have interposed some measure of judicial safeguard after all is as yet uncertain. In that case *(In re Article 26 of the Constitution and the Emergency Powers Bill, 1976)* the court went out of its way to refute the claim of the Attorney General that once the Oireachtas resolutions have been passed, the Court has no jurisdiction to review their content. 'The court expressly reserves for future consideration the question whether the courts have jurisdiction to review such resolutions.'[2]

Bunreacht na hEireann also contains one article, Article 45 entitled 'Directive Principles of Social Policy', that includes a limitation on the power of the courts to review. This article is explicitly addressed to the members of the Oireachtas:

> The principles of social policy set forth in this Article are intended for the general guidance of the Oireachtas. The application of those principles in the making of laws shall be the care of the Oireachtas exclusively, and shall not be cognisable by any court under any of the provisions of this Constitution.

The apparent finality of this wording was underlined by the fact that de Valera made it abundantly clear in the Dáil debates on the draft Constitution that 'it is the Legislature that must determine how far it can go from time to time ... in trying to secure these ideals and aims and objectives'.[3] Nevertheless, some judges in the seventies took the view that the Directive Principles, which comprise a set of 'welfare state' aims, might after all be looked at in considering whether a constitutional right existed. Clearly this raises an important question about the role of the courts which might in some circumstances become a live political issue, and we shall return to it below (see pp. 74 ff.).

Finally, mention must be made of another kind of limitation. When Ireland became a member of the European Communities, the Treaties themselves became part of the domestic law of the state. Article 177 of the Treaty establishing the European Economic Community, like Article 150 of the Euratom Treaty, gave the Court of Justice of the Communities jurisdiction to interpret the Treaties for national courts. To what extent this limits the jurisdiction of national courts is as yet far from clear. In the case of *Campus Oil Ltd. and Others v. Minister for Industry and Energy* ([1983] I.R. 82), the Supreme Court ruled that Article 177 'confers upon an Irish national judge an unfettered discretion to make a preliminary reference to the Court of Justice for an interpretation of the Treaty ... to fetter that right, by making it subject to review on appeal, would be contrary to both the spirit and the letter of Article 177 of the Treaty.'[4] The appellate jurisdiction of the Supreme Court therefore does not include jurisdiction to entertain an appeal from the decision of a High Court judge to request a ruling on the interpretation of the Treaty: in itself a tiny chink perhaps, but none the less significant.

These powers of the High Court and the Supreme Court to *review* for constitutionality obviously give them the opportunity to *interpret* the Constitution, but how far can they *change* it? They are clearly limited:

> Courts it must be emphasised cannot amend a Constitution. They must accept the words, and so far as they introduce change, it can come only through their interpretation of the meaning of the words. Courts may, by a series of decisions, elaborate the content of a word or phrase; they may even revoke or contradict previous decisions.[5]

The wording of a clause might be such that there is room for judges to supply from their own minds what the constitution makers might have meant or implied. Going further, they might interpret a provision in a contemporary context, very different perhaps from the conditions that obtained when the constitution was framed. Thus they come to develop the constitution which, as we have suggested, consists of both a document and an ever-increasing penumbra of authoritative principles and rules added item by item as cases arise. Such a penumbra might according to the circumstances of a state consist of comparatively few accretions clinging closely to the core, i.e. the words of the document, or they could be numerous and wide-ranging. What has been the Irish experience?

II

It is not intended here to review systematically the cases involving constitutional interpretation that have come before the High Court and the Supreme Court.[6] Rather, we are concerned, first, with the great and continuing increase in the number of cases which has been a feature since the middle sixties and, second, with the general thrust of the judgements delivered by the courts. On account of both, the courts have been drawn much more towards the centre of the political stage and these developments have important political implications and raise contentious political issues.

In the years following the inception of *Bunreacht na hEireann*, up to the early sixties, there were few cases and there is general agreement among legal writers on this subject that, in the cases that did arise, most of the judges took up what one of them characterised as 'a narrow rather inflexible approach to constitutional interpretation, with emphasis on harsh construction and reading down of the constitutional provisions in question.'[7] They were 'rarely innovatory.' Another went further, remarking on the tendency of the judges of that period 'to tiptoe around judicial review.'[8]

This approach is easily explained. Judicial review of this kind was new to Ireland: it was in fact foreign to the traditions in which the lawyers of the time had been trained and had practised. They were slow to recognize and exploit the opportunities opened up by *Bunreacht na hEireann*. Nor was there any tradition of private citizens instituting court cases on constitutional points. The plaintiff in *O'Donovan* v. *Attorney General,* ([1961] I.R. 114), a constituency boundaries case of considerable political consequence, was an important exception when he took this step. Also, many lawyers knew that de Valera took a narrow view of the functions and role of the courts and they were as uneasy about him as he was suspicious of them. In the debate on the draft Constitution, he pointedly extended his remarks on the modest role of judges to cover not only Article 45 but the rights articles and the Constitution generally. It has to be remembered, too, that the Irish state, born in civil war, was continuously plagued by subversive organizations and shortly after *Bunreacht na hEireann* was enacted was once again in a period of emergency when the war in Europe broke out. It seemed to be a time for strong government rather than enlarging citizens' rights.

When constitutional cases did arise, the practitioners, trained in the British system with its emphasis on the common law, the sovereignty of parliament and judicial precedent, were chary of making creative use of the new powers bestowed upon the courts, let alone of adopting a 'policy-oriented' approach in the manner of some American courts. Judges tended to interpret the rights of the citizen conservatively, to give judgements that bestowed considerable powers and discretion on governments and to leave the extension of social and economic rights to the Oireachtas. In 1940, the Supreme Court declared that:

> the duty of determining the extent to which the rights of any particular citizen, or class of citizens, can properly be harmonized with the rights of the citizens as a whole seems to us to be a matter which is peculiarly within the province of the Oireachtas, and any attempt by this Court to control the Oireachtas in the exercise of this function would, in our opinion, be a usurpation of its authority. [9]

Likewise, in the previous year, Mr Justice Hanna in the High Court had baulked at being asked to interpret the phrase 'peace, order and good government' and the term 'social justice'. The first he dubbed 'a kind of political shibboleth', a matter for 'practical political science'; the second:

> a nebulous phrase, involving no question of law for the Courts, but questions of ethics, morals, economics and sociology which are, in my opinion, beyond the determination of a court of law, but which may be, in their various aspects, within the consideration of the Oireachtas, as representing the people, when framing the law. [10]

The courts would of course do their duty in seeing that the legislature did not transgress constitutional limits.

Not all the judges in the early days of the state were of this mind. In the twenties and thirties, Chief Justice Kennedy, one of the drafters of the Irish Free State Constitution, and following him Mr Justice Gavan Duffy, were minority voices among their more conservative colleagues. Significantly, they were also, as Gerard Hogan put it, 'undoubtedly the most nationalistically minded of all the judges appointed in the first thirty years of the state.' Both 'aspired after a distinctly Irish legal system' and 'sensed that the creation of a native constitutional jurisprudence would assist in that development.'[11] Significantly also — and attention has already been drawn to this (p. 42-44 above) — it was to the natural law that they turned as one of the principal bases for such a native jurisprudence. They were lone voices in their day, but when the climate changed these were to be among the most prominent features of the development of Irish constitutional jurisprudence.

By the middle 1960s the climate had changed. In the second edition of his authoritative *Fundamental Rights in The Irish Law and Constitution,* published in 1967, J. M. Kelly noted that the number of cases coming before the courts had been 'progressively increasing' and, in his view, 'judicial interpretation has been increasingly bold.'[12] Many writers see the appointment of Cearbhall Ó Dálaigh to be Chief Justice in 1961 as heralding 'the beginning of a new era in Irish jurisprudence.'[13] Some tend to speak of 'the Ó Dálaigh Court', as American writers do of 'the Warren Court', the great reforming and innovative Supreme Court of the United States in the fifties and sixties, but this is misleading. The judges of the Supreme Court of that time were not all of the same mind and this would usually be the case. Besides, judges come and go. Likewise, in the High Court: it was a judge of that Court, Mr Justice Kenny, whose decision in the case of *Ryan* v. *Attorney General,* ([1965] I.R. 294) is universally recognized as a seminal judgement, introducing as it did the new concept of 'undisclosed human rights'. Others of his colleagues though were more conservative.

This 'new era' was partly the result of a generational change at the Bar and partly the fruits of a learning process. The legal profession had become more familiar with the new constitutional situation and those entering it were arriving progressively better trained and equipped. This trend has continued and, with a veritable 'litigation explosion' as one writer has called it,[14] the profession has become larger, livelier, more sophisticated and exhibiting a greater propensity to seek authorities from a wider range of sources than hitherto. These changes were, though, but part of a more general change in Irish society that led to the sixties being characterized as a 'decade of upheaval'. As the community at last dragged itself out of the stagnation of the post-World War II, de Valera period, the pace of social, economic and cultural change was unprecedented in Irish experience. The legal profession and the courts were inevitably caught up in it in a process of growth and change that has now continued for more than a quarter of a century.

The courts' opportunities to develop the Constitution are governed by the cases brought before them. In the first twenty-five years after the enactment of *Bunreacht na hEireann* there were very few, on average two or three a year.[15] In the next twenty-five years they increased dramatically. Concentrating solely on 'major cases challenging the constitutionality of legislation enacted since 1937', Chief Justice Finlay found that 'between 1937 and 1970 there were only 13 major challenges, but between 1971 and 1987 there had been a further 45.'[16]

This increase was partly due to the courts' apparent willingness to be innovative for it encouraged potential litigants to try their luck. That willingness, however, involved an important change in the judges' attitude towards the decisions of their predecessors. A necessary preliminary to an innovative approach in deciding cases was to abandon a strict doctrine of precedent, to which hitherto the Courts had considered themselves bound in constitutional cases except for the most compelling reasons. Judgements in the sixties relaxed the principle and gave the necessary flexibility. By the end of the seventies it was the view of a leading constitutional lawyer that 'the Supreme Court's attitude to precedent now conforms to that of constitutional courts in other countries such as Australia and the United States.'[17]

Likewise, the judges who were prone to take a broader approach to interpreting the Constitution began to look more widely for guidance as to what the law should be than their predecessors had. Recourse was had to the Preamble to *Bunreacht na hEireann* and, as we have already noted, to Article 45 (the Directive Principles of Social Policy). Going further, some judges began to infer from the wording and the general tenor of the Constitution what Chief Justice O'Higgins called 'basic doctrines of political and social theory'.[18] Applying principles based on such doctrines led them in particular to deduce or discover unmentioned, and hitherto unrecognized, rights. In 1965, in the case of *Ryan v. Attorney General,* Mr Justice Kenny gave it as his opinion that:

> the personal rights which may be invoked to invalidate legislation are not confined to those specified in Article 40 but include all those rights which result from the Christian and democratic nature of the state.[19]

This line of thought, which received considerable support from his colleagues and initiated a whole new genre of constitional rights, contrasted markedly with the opinions of most of the judges of a previous generation, epitomised by Mr Justice Johnston in a judgement twenty five years before:

> I do not think that a further Constitution — an unwritten one — was intended by the People of Eire to exist side by side with this written Constitution or even — perhaps it would be more correct to say — outside and beyond the present Constitution.[20]

Ó Dálaigh, Kenny and their colleagues were moving fast into unknown territory, the more so since, as was increasingly the case, they also rejected an historical approach to interpretation. This view was well expressed later — though by no means for the first time — by Mr Justice McCarthy in *Norris* v. *Attorney General:*

> I find it philosophically impossible to carry out the necessary exercise of applying what I might believe to be the thinking of 1937 to the demands of 1983 . . . I cannot accept the approach based upon applying the test of the then contemporary mores to the issue of constitutionality.[21]

III

The results of the judges and of lawyers generally developing this approach were — and continue to be — far-reaching, the more so because the development of a new jurisprudence of this kind has the character of a progression. New possibilities lead to more litigation, which leads to further exploration and the opening up of new territory, which in turn reveals yet more possibilities. This was certainly the experience in a number of areas of law including human rights and constitutional justice, which are of particular importance for this study.

By 1974, Mr Justice Walsh was arguing (in *McGee* v. *Attorney General*) that:

> Articles 41, 42 and 43 emphatically reject the theory that there are no rights without laws, no rights contrary to the law and no rights anterior to the law. They indicate that justice is placed above the law and acknowledge that natural rights or human rights are not created by law but that the Constitution can confirm their existence and give them protection.[22]

An unprecedented number of cases were by then being brought to the courts and gave him and his colleagues the opportunity to use the Constitution for this purpose. A distinguished constitutional lawyer commented at the time that 'the speed with which new unspecified rights can be recognized and enforced is startling.'[23] He listed nine, among them advances in areas of fundamental importance such as the right to bodily integrity, the right to work, the right to belong to a trade union, the right to a career, the right to free movement and the right to marry. This spate of discovering rights has since abated; but they continue to be identified from time to time as cases are brought, among them important ones such as a general right to privacy, the right to communicate and the right of a trade union member to take part in the decision-making processes of his union within its rules. Of significance also, the Supreme Court (in *Meskell* v. *CIE* [1973] I.R. 121) made clear, where the constitution is silent, that a right guaranteed by the Constitution can be pursued by an action for damages.

Equally important, procedural safeguards and personal rights in respect of litigation and the treatment of accused persons also began to be formulated or redefined. From the middle sixties the term 'constitutional justice' began to be used by some Irish lawyers to describe this area of human rights. As they saw it, satisfactory conditions in respect of these matters were an essential complement of just laws and their implementation, and the courts began to identify and expand rights in this category. Generalizing in 1976, Mr Justice Henchy gave his view of what 'the extended ambit' of the term constitutional justice covered in addition to the two basic and well-established principles of *audi alteram partem* (both sides of the case must be heard) and *nemo iudex in causa sua* (no man shall be judge in his own case):

> The necessary implementation of express or necessarily implied constitutional guarantees means that decisive acts and procedures may be impugned for a wide variety of reasons depending on the circumstances of the case; for instance, because justice was not administered in public; or the decision applied an unconstitutional law; or the accused was deprived of a fair, competent and impartial jury; or the person affected received unjustifiable unequal treatment; or the evidence was obtained in a manner not constitutionally permissible. [24]

This avenue was also used to broaden access to the courts. There was a succession of important cases in the middle sixties. *The State (Quinn) v. Ryan and Others* ([1965] I.R. 70) concerned the right to unhampered access to the courts to question the validity of a warrant. In *MacCauley v. The Minister for Posts and Telegraphs* ([1966] I.R. 345) it was held that the requirement to have the *fiat* of the Attorney General in order to proceed against a minister impeded the constitutional right of access to the courts. Likewise, *Byrne v. Ireland and the Attorney General* ([1972] I.R. 24) finally disposed of the immunity claimed by the state on the ground that it had inherited the former prerogative of the British Crown (i.e. government) making it immune from being sued for a civil wrong. As a result of this and many other cases '[the] capacity of the state to be sued as such (i.e. as 'Ireland') is now beyond doubt.'[25]

A similar whittling away process took place in respect of state claims to the privilege of not disclosing information and, in the same vein, the courts have effected improvements in the way people are treated by the Garda and other officials before, during and after court hearings. Likewise, more recently, the Supreme Court (in *Costello v. Director of Public Prosecutions* [1984] I.R. 436) declared unconstitutional the power of the Director of Public Prosecutions to send a person for trial after the District Court had held that there was no case to answer. It can now be said that the strong tendency of the courts to constitutionalize the right to a fair hearing has gone a long way 'in creating an Irish analogue of the fertile Due Process clauses of the United States Constitution.'[26]

An inevitable consequence of the judges' increasing propensity to operationalize citizens' rights was that they more and more interfered with the activities of other organs of government. They sought to ensure that other authorities observed the Constitution even when the law purported to give them unfettered discretion and in spite of the strongly established principle that a law passed by the Oireachtas is presumed to be constitutional unless the contrary is clearly established.[27] The lengths to which they were prepared to go were dramatically illustrated in 1987. In the important case of *Crotty* v. *An Taoiseach,* a majority of the Supreme Court held that the power of the government to make policy is subject to limits and is reviewable. It was not entitled to enter into arrangements which restricted its own freedom to decide matters of foreign policy.[28]

Developments of this sort might be viewed as an inevitable consequence of the adoption of a Constitution providing for judicial review, the only call for comment being the length of time it took the legal profession and the public generally to realize the potential of *Bunreacht na hEireann.* Is there not more to it than this however? Perhaps the burgeoning propensity of the judges to innovate in the last quarter century reflects, as Gerard Hogan put it, a 'desire on the part of many senior members of the Irish judiciary to enhance the distinctiveness of Irish law.'[29] He wrote of a 'wish to de-anglicize the Irish legal system, and to create an indigenous body of law.'[30] An overwhelming majority of the judges of the forties and fifties, because of their backgrounds and political views, did not feel this need: their successors, people of a different generation and appointed by a different government, did. Ó Dálaigh and some of his colleagues in the early sixties were determined to make a fresh start and to release the Irish legal system from the English. McMahon expressed it thus: 'We were different; other countries could express their uniqueness with distinctive individuality, and there was no reason why we too, as a legal system, could not move out from under the colonial shadow and go it alone.'[31] This was Irish nationalism displaying itself — belatedly some might think — in yet another aspect of social life and in another form, in Hogan's phrase, as 'a legal ideology'.[32]

There might be argument about the extent to which these developments have reflected a self-conscious desire to 'de-anglicize' the law rather than an inevitable organic growth of a new jurisprudence consequent upon the adoption of a new constitution and the process of developing it. What cannot be doubted is that the establishment in Hogan's words of:

what may be described as a 'native Irish common law' has largely been achieved through the infusion of constitutional principles into standard legal concepts. Already, the influence of constitutional principles has had a major impact on subjects such as administrative law, evidence and tort and there are indications that these principles will prove to be significant in areas such as contract and labour law. [34]

IV

The increasing willingness of the courts to interpret *Bunreacht na hEireann* imaginatively together with the great growth in the number of cases which has been both the occasion and the consequence of this, has greatly increased the judges' contribution to constitutional development. They have emerged to fill what had been a constitutional void. This trend in the practice of Irish law is clearly in principle beneficial for it helps keep fundamental law in touch with the needs and values of the community and thus contributes to maintaining the normative character of the Constitution. Nevertheless, it has its potential dangers.

To begin with, the judges' search for principles on which to base implied and hitherto 'undisclosed' rights has led them into uncharted territory, each drawing his own map. The appeal — in the search for authority — to the words of the Preamble and to the Directive Principles of Social Policy in Article 45, which had at first been regarded as being not justiciable, caused little difficulty. However, when judges began to draw authority from less specific sources, they were treading on softer ground altogether. Working in the cultural context of a Catholic country, it was perhaps inevitable that natural law and natural rights derived therefrom should be invoked: in any case, in *Bunreacht na hEireann* itself reference is made to natural rights and implicitly to the natural law whence they are derived. Indeed, Pope Pius XII himself congratulated de Valera on the fact that the human rights formulations in *Bunreacht na hEireann* were 'grounded on the bedrock of the natural law'.[35] Chief Justice Kennedy, as we have noted, had earlier invoked it in the context of the Irish Free State Constitution and Gavan Duffy had lost no time in using it in interpreting *Bunreacht na hEireann* to strike down rules made within the traditional parameters of British

law. In the path-breaking judgement in *Ryan* v. *Attorney General*
in which he enunciated the concept of 'undisclosed' human rights,
Mr Justice Kenny spoke of the Christian and democratic nature
of the Constitution but, more pointedly, cited a Papal Encyclical.
Others followed him.[36]

However, as Desmond Clarke has shown, Irish judges seem
to have used the word natural in a variety of ways and to have
floundered between a number of 'natural law' theories. '"Natural
law" is interpreted in such a way that mutually incompatible decisions
are held to be derived from [it] even by justices with a broadly
common cultural and legal background... [it] only provides the
illusion of specific guidance on detailed matters of human
rights....'[37] What is more, 'there is a danger, at least in theory,
in muddled natural law thinking obscuring the extent to which the
purely personal views of members of the judiciary might be
substituted for legislation which has been democratically enacted
by the Oireachtas.'[38] This was even more the case with the subsequent
appeals by Irish judges to yet vaguer (if superficially attractive)
principles on which to base the enunciation of a rule or a right
such as 'the Christian and democratic nature of the state', 'prudence,
justice and charity', and 'human personality'. It could go further.
Mr Justice Brian Walsh expressed the view — thankfully not in
the context of a legal judgement — that:

> the social philosophy of much of the Constitution, and indeed
> the recognition of human or natural rights, while corresponding
> to the Christian ethic, cannot be solely attributed to
> Christianity, much less to a particular Christian church. The
> Constitution steers a middle course between a wholly humanist
> type of common good and a transpersonalistic one.[39]

As early as 1967, Professor J. M. Kelly was arguing that this kind
of approach 'introduces into our law an element of uncertainty,
and thus an element which is repugnant to the central value of
the very concept of law itself.'[40] As he pointed out, the Oireachtas
itself could not know for sure what rights it must respect or could
delimit. Likewise, it became difficult for lawyers to give reliable
advice to their clients in some rights issues. By 1980, one academic
lawyer could say that 'in large areas, they can no longer do so
as a result of the danger that some law will be struck down for
unconstitutionality. The feelings of exasperation and cynicism in

the legal profession are such that Senior Counsel talk about "losing in the High Court and then going on to Disneyland".[41]

A consequence of this state of affairs was that the courts began increasingly to be seen as the place to which those with a grievance or a cause could resort when the politicians would not act. For a decade or so from the middle sixties it fell to the courts to introduce up-dating reforms in the high visibility area of civil liberties. Inevitably such decisions attracted publicity and the courts began to receive more media attention and journalistic comment than before. In particular, cases establishing the right of women to act as jurors (*de Burca* v. *Attorney General* [1976] I.R.38]) the right to privacy in marital matters, i.e. to acquire contraceptives, (*McGee* v. *Attorney General* [1974] I.R.284), the right of married people to be taxed separately (*Murphy* v. *Attorney General* [1982] I.R. 241) brought the courts into the public eye and evoked a favourable response. According to one writer, the judiciary had become 'the protector of individual liberty against state excesses: ... we have been fortunate in having had, by and large a liberal, courageous and increasingly self-reliant judiciary ....'[42] The judges were praised for having the courage to do what the politicians were failing to do or could be prevented by pressure from doing.

If some judgements attracted favourable comment from liberals, not least those in the media, others, notably in property rights cases, were seen rightly or wrongly as restrictive and conservative. Some, too, were, as R.F.V. Heuston delicately put it, 'exceedingly inconvenient from an administrative point of view.'[43] Some decisions in electoral law, and in social welfare and tax law cases, for example, were of this sort. Even more exasperating for the authorities were decisions affecting the rights of accused persons and the power of the police, in particular the judgement in the O'Callaghan case (*People* v. *O'Callaghan* [1966] I.R. 501) which greatly increased the likelihood of accused persons getting bail. Above all, the decision of the Supreme Court in *Crotty* v. *An Taoiseach* in April 1987, that the government was not entitled to ratify a treaty that restricted the freedom of future government to decide matters of foreign policy — a decision which obliged it to submit its proposal to ratify the Single European Act to a referendum — evoked an outburst of criticism from leading politicians.[44] What was always inherent in the development of a more innovative judiciary was by 1987 starkly evident: the judges had come onto the political stage. When some kinds of cases were brought before them, they might find themselves at its very centre. Clearly, there were in this development potential dangers for the judiciary as an institution which in Ireland had hitherto seemed remote.

Although the courts are for very good reasons set apart from the other institutions of government and intentionally, even ostentatiously, insulated from politics, the power to review for constitutionality might on occasion open the reviewing judge or judges to political comment. The identity of the parties, the nature of the case, the surrounding circumstances, above all the court's decision — any or all of these might evoke partisan comment. It cannot be helped: the courts have a duty to process the cases brought before them. What is more, it has to be recognized and accepted that judicial decisions, though given to decide only the case before the court, in some cases inevitably have wide-ranging consequences and an important effect upon what comes after. Judgements in the courts can and do affect the way government and administration are carried on, and they change or make public policy. Most judicial contributions are negative in the sense that the courts veto what they perceive to be unconstitutional action by other branches of government. Such decisions do not usually raise questions about the impartiality of the judges. The perception of objectivity is the greater if judicial decisions flow from accepted sources of law, are grounded in or developed from precedents, and are arrived at according to the accepted standards by which lawyers operate.

The more judges deliver reforming and innovative judgements, particularly if they base their rulings on abstract concepts or principles that are novel, the more likely are their decisions to evoke political comment, not least when their rulings have important policy implications. The same will happen if they seem to be showing a propensity to challenge or curb other authorities. In these circumstances, their role in the system and their relationship with other institutions of government can soon come into question, and not only their role but more personal aspects such as their backgrounds, their personalities, and their social attitudes. In this regard, the experience of the Supreme Court of the United States of America is instructive, although admittedly there are great differences between the traditions and demeanour of the two court systems and their propensity to get involved in policy formulation. The Supreme Court under Chief Justice Warren in the fifties and sixties took a much more positive stance than its predecessors and issued a succession of innovative judgements in constitutional cases. It came to be seen by politicians and public alike as an instrument of social reform not least in such controversial areas as desegregation in schools and the drawing of electoral boundaries. In any case, appointments to the Court had long been the object of political interest and partisan action. According to the distinguished American lawyer, Archibald Cox, 'the Chief Justiceship of Earl Warren brought a period of extraordinary creativity in constitutional law which ... greatly enlarged the role of the Supreme Court in American government and further politicized the process of constitutional adjudication.'[45] More recently, the rejection by the Senate of President Reagan's nominee, Judge Robert Bork, because of his opinions on social issues showed how far political partisanship can go in the United States.

Cox points to the danger of two undesirable consequences of increased judicial 'activism', as he calls it:

> First, there is concern that the Court may sacrifice the power of legitimacy that attaches to decisions within the traditional judicial sphere rendered on the basis of conventional legal criteria, and so may disable itself from performing the narrower but none the less vital constitutional role that all assign to it. Second, there is a fear that excessive reliance upon courts instead of self-government through democratic processes may deaden a people's sense of moral and political responsibility for their own future, especially in matters of liberty, and may stunt the growth of political capacity that results from the exercise of ultimate power of decision.[46]

No-one would suggest that the Irish courts have come anywhere near emulating the Supreme Court of the United States as policy makers or reformers. Nor is this likely, but recent experience has shown both how easily Irish judges can go at least a short distance down this road and also how quickly such a move might endanger 'the power of legitimacy'. The Irish High Court and the Supreme Court *did have*, to borrow Cox's words, 'a period of extraordinary creativity in constitutional law', they *have* 'greatly enlarged their role'; and people *have* begun to comment in a partisan manner.

Mention was made above of one powerful pressure group (PLAC) moving to forestall anticipated court decisions of a reforming kind by getting legislation which they thought might be threatened, underpinned by constitutional amendment.[47] The courts in their view needed to be curbed. More recently, however, they have come under attack from the opposite camp. After a period of adulation of the courts by liberals some judges have evoked criticism from them. In cases like *Norris* v. *Attorney General* ([1984] I.R. 36) and *Crotty* v. *An Taoiseach* ([1987] 2 C.M.L.R. 657) the views of three supposedly conservative Supreme Court judges have been contrasted with the sentiments of an apparently progressive two. Is it too fanciful to foresee, were there a succession of cases involving socially or politically sensitive issues, the judges concerned coming under considerable partisan criticism in a spate of dubbing members of the judiciary 'conservative' or 'liberal', 'nationalist' or 'anti-nationalist', 'sectarian' or 'secular'? The treatment accorded to the former Chief Justice Ó Dálaigh, when as President he exercised his undoubted constitutional right to refer the Emergency Powers Bill, 1976 to the Supreme Court for a ruling on whether its provisions were constitutional, suggests that it is not. Likewise, in extradition cases involving people wanted or convicted for terrorist crimes in Northern Ireland, the statements of some judges concerned evoked critical comment.[48] Is it wholly out of the question that an exasperated government in the future might pay much closer attention than hitherto to the record, opinions and attitudes of possible candidates for senior judicial posts, looking for people likely to deliver the 'right' kind of judgements? It is undesirable enough that the government should have such posts in their giving in any case: it would be an unhappy day were a Judge-Bork-type appraisal to become part of the nominating process.

Archibald Cox's second concern — about the stultifying effect of 'excessive reliance upon courts instead of self-government through democratic processes' — might also be thought to have relevance in Ireland. In fact it has occurred. It was the courts from the middle sixties which enlarged the rights of the citizens in a manner arguably reflecting the changing needs and values of the community. It was the courts — in the *McGee* case — which made a radical change in the law relating to contraceptives, a change which in Hogan's view 'could not then have been brought through the ordinary legislative process.'[49] Subsequent events demonstrated that politicians were not even then prepared to grapple with the demands of the resultant situation for a decade. Again, it was a court decision — in the case of *M.* v. *An Bord Uchtála* ([1975] I.R. 81) — that circumvented what a minister euphemistically called 'a stone wall', i.e. the veto of the Catholic Hierarchy, blocking changes in the law on adoption, and opened the way to a much-needed reform.[50] By the middle seventies, as Hogan put it, 'it was recognized on all sides that the possibility of social reform via constitutional test cases had widened the parameters of any debate on what came to be known as the social issues: contraception, abortion, homosexuality and illegitimacy.'[51]

Such a development might on occasions suit politicians, but many court decisions of this kind have wide social consequences. Inevitably they have the character of quasi-legislative decrees but, because of their source, 'cannot be said like true legislation to have the legitimacy which flows from the processes of democratic self-government.'[52] It is the democratically elected representatives of the people who should be making public policy. It is for the government to formulate and propose policy and for the Oireachtas, by assenting to the proposals, to legitimate them. It is they who should be the architects of significant constitutional development, taking care in their work to match the direction and pace of change with cultural changes in the community. The apparatus of election, representation and the parliamentary process is designed to ensure responsive leadership and to punish by removal those who fail to satisfy their constituents. Unfortunately, it has sometimes been the case that politicians have been unwilling or slow to shoulder their responsibilities: that is another matter and we shall return to it (see chapter 9 below).

The courts are on the periphery of this system. Clearly, their functions thrust them into the role of developers of the Constitution. Equally clearly, it is right that they should apply contemporary standards, and reflect changes in those standards. Nevertheless, it has to be recognized that as a class judges are not obviously the best-fitted people — harsher critics might say that they are not even well-fitted — to identify and appreciate the changes in the 'consensus' in the community, a term which a former British judge, Lord Devlin, defined as those ideas 'which its members as a whole like or, if they dislike, will submit to — what is for one reason or another acceptable.'[53] It follows that they should develop the Constitution in a cautious, even cagey, manner, nurturing carefully the belief that the community by and large holds, that their decisions 'are based on impartial judgement justifiable primarily in terms of the legal materials available to them.'[54] It is desirable, even perhaps necessary, to discourage, in the words of Mr Justice Brian Walsh, 'the transformation of forensic bricklayers into social architects.'[55]

── 7 ──

Northern Ireland and the Constitution

BUNREACHT NA hEIREANN, like its predecessors, can appropriately be viewed as marking a stage in the evolution of the country's relationship with the United Kingdom. Would it, however, accommodate the next — and hopefully final — stage? De Valera was right in his belief that he had so fashioned it that it would not need to be changed when it became practicable formally to declare the twenty-six-county state a republic. He was wrong, as we can now in retrospect see clearly, in believing that it could also accommodate the addition of the other six counties. His strategy for handling the Northern problem was to relegate it to 'the back burner' while he grappled with what he called 'the big question'[1]. However, this had the effect of masking the unsuitability of some of the provisions of the Constitution for an all-Ireland state, for the basic law of which it purported to provide at some unspecified time in the future. He thus postponed an inevitable encounter with reality.

It is one of the ironies of Irish history that when 'the big question' was solved — by the changes made in 1948 and 1949 — the result was the opposite of what the Irish leaders who made them expressly hoped, namely that this would 'take the gun out of Irish politics'. On the contrary, it made way for the advancement of the Northern problem from the back burner to the forefront of Anglo-Irish relations where it has since simmered and occasionally boiled over.

Increasing concern about the position of the Northern Catholic minority was accompanied by a slowly growing awareness that the heart of the problem is the existence on the island not of one community with a dissident minority, but of two communities each with its own traditions, loyalties and aspirations, and that the laws and governmental practices of the Republic embodied the values of only one of these communities while ignoring those of the other. This learning process was painfully slow, for it involved questioning and rejecting basic nationalist myths. From the middle sixties, however, a growing number of people began to accept that, contrary to de Valera's view, any solution of the Northern problem would require the amendment or replacement of *Bunreacht na hEireann.* Thus, Ireland's next constitution, like all its predecessors, might be occasioned by a change — actual, intended or putative — in the status of Northern Ireland. At the very least, important amendments would be required in the present Constitution, *Bunreacht na hEireann.* The nature, extent and timing of such changes became and remained a political issue.

Action in and by the Republic cannot, however, of itself solve the problem, nor can the two sovereign governments individually or together impose a solution upon Northern Ireland willy-nilly. For any solution to be reached, a complex collection of agreed constitutional changes involving Northern Ireland, the United Kingdom and the Republic would be needed. The pages of recent Irish and British constitutional history are littered with statements of irreconcilable positions and failed initiatives that bear witness to the attempts to get the process under way. They show how little the governments and people of the Republic have been prepared to concede to the other tradition. They show, too, how even yet the utter determination of most Unionists not to join an all-Ireland republic on any terms nor to contemplate arrangements that look like steps on the road to such a state, and their ability to veto any changes of this kind, have not been fully recognized, let alone accepted, by many of the Republic's political leaders or the mass of the people. Politicians still proclaim objectives that have no hope of being achieved in the foreseeable future. Because of this and because the Republic, as we shall see, now does have a role in policy making for Northern Ireland, it continues to be a context within which changes in *Bunreacht na hEireann* are advocated and debated. It is the purpose of this chapter to trace the learning process that is as yet incomplete, and to discuss the constitutional issues that are raised by the prospect, however unlikely, of changes in the status of Northern Ireland.

II

As far as the six counties were concerned, *Bunreacht na hEireann* sought to formalize in law the nationalist position on partition. Since the objective of unity was not as yet realized, the Constitution was, in John Kelly's words, 'conceived in part as a manifesto rather than as bare law.'[2] That position rested on a number of 'myths', in the sociological meaning of that word, i.e. value-bestowing beliefs and explanations. They included the belief that the people of Ireland were one nation; that the national territory comprised the whole island; that its partition, which was imposed by the United Kingdom, would inevitably be undone; and that a politically reunited all-Ireland state would emerge.[3] Nationalists believed that when the United Kingdom eventually moved to undo the wrong it had done and Ulster Unionists were obliged to come into an all-Ireland state, which if necessary they could be forced to do by the British, very little if any change in the Constitution would be needed. Article 2 defined the national territory as the whole island: Article 3 envisaged reintegration': and Article 15 2.2[0] made provision 'for the creation or recognition of subordinate legislatures and for the powers and functions of these legislatures', thus providing for the inclusion of Stormont, the Northern Ireland regional parliament.

The enormity of the internal contradictions in a Constitution that purported to serve an all-Ireland state, yet which so clearly accommodated only the values of the Republican, Catholic, Gaelic tradition was not recognized by de Valera and those — the vast majority — who accepted the nationalist myths which he had done so much to inculcate in them. Because the nationalist frame of reference included a woefully inadequate concept of Ulster Unionism, people simply did not take realistic account of the views of the million and more Northern Protestants, let alone accord them value. Many Southern leaders, not least de Valera himself, had little acquaintance with the North. Looking back in 1972, Eoin Ryan, a senior and much respected Fianna Fáil Senator, said openly what many had said in private: 'For some reason, Dev. never quite got the wavelength of the North — Unionists or Nationalists.'[4] The same could have been said of many people in the South.

During the Dáil debate on the draft Constitution in 1937, Frank McDermott, an Independent Deputy, put it to de Valera that:

to achieve unity we have got to offer them [Northern Protestants] an Ireland in which a place can be found for their traditions and aspirations as well as ours. Until we are willing to do this we are partitionists at heart, no matter how loudly we shout about unity.[5]

His was almost a lone voice crying in the wilderness. It took thirty years for the validity of this view to be widely enough accepted for politicians to take it up. It was not until the late sixties that people in any numbers began to question and discard the traditional nationalist myths. Then, the concept of 'the two traditions' began to evolve and the view to be expressed that both being Irish, both must be accommodated. To attempt an accommodation would involve contemplating the proposition that unity could only come with the consent of the Protestant minority; abandoning the claims in Articles 2 and 3; discarding that part of Article 44 which accorded the Roman Catholic Church a special position; and modifying constitutional provisions and other legislation on moral issues like divorce and abortion and on education. This was a truly formidable agenda and politicians were understandably slow to accept it and, even when they did, were reluctant to take it up.

III

Revisionism can be a dangerous business for politicians, particularly where deeply held beliefs are involved. It takes courage, and to be successful, requires an acute sense of timing. Paradoxically, a messianic leader who is himself identified with the orthodoxy that is coming into question, is better placed, if he can bring himself to contemplate it, to induce a change of direction than those who follow him. De Valera, we have argued, did not appreciate some of the essential facts of the Northern situation but, as John Bowman has shown, he was 'pragmatic' in his approach, and sometimes 'heretical' and 'revisionist'.[6] He expressed himself willing on occasions to recognize that Unionists could not, and should not, be forced into an all-Ireland state; to accord a measure of autonomy to the North, even perhaps a federal arrangement; to allow the people of each county to opt for which region they wished to join;

and to develop an 'external association' with the United Kingdom. However, because it never seemed to him to be opportune to make or respond to a move, he never had to face up to the question of actually amending his Constitution and — what would also be necessary — taking on the extreme nationalist wing of his party.

The consequence of de Valera's cautious, even cagey, approach and the growing conservatism of his ageing regime and of Ireland generally was that his Constitution developed the rock-like qualities of Moses' tablets. The acid test applied to his successors' policies and pronouncements was the orthodoxies contained in it. To the rank and file in his party, as to many others, Articles 2 and 3 in particular were sacrosanct. No minority had the right to thwart the attainment of the ultimate objective, which, like Parnell, they saw as the march of a nation. By the middle nineteen sixties, however, de Valera's successor, Seán Lemass, who was both a pragmatic and a decisive man, recognized that if there was to be any movement, the Unionist position would have to be taken into account and policies adjusted to meet it. Some of the younger generation in the party like Jack Lynch and George Colley had no doubt of it. Lynch, Lemass's successor, thought that the principles on which the Constitution was based were 'narrower and less generous' than those of 'the original nationalist position': it was 'not suitable for a new Ireland'.[7] So, too, in the Fine Gael Party where also, as in Fianna Fáil, there were traditionalists and revisionists. Northern policy and constitutional change were important issues in causing the rifts and the formation of rival factions that accompanied the attempts at modernization in both these parties at this time.

The wide divergence of views among politicians on these issues was well illustrated by the experiences of the Lemass-inspired Committee on the Constitution which reported in 1967 and its more shadowy successor, of 1972. The first, the Committee on the Constitution, was remarkable both for the progressive views it expressed on a number of constitutional issues and for its complete misjudgement of what was politically possible at that time. Revisionists dominated the Committee and it was common ground among them that some parts of the Constitution were a positive hindrance to achieving unity. If there was ever to be a hope of this, those articles that gave offence to Northern Unionists or aroused apprehensions would have to be amended.

On Article 3 the members made a unanimous recommendation. They reported that:

> it would now be appropriate to adopt a new provision to replace Article 3. The wording which we would suggest is as follows:

> 1. The Irish Nation hereby proclaims its firm will that its territory be re-united in harmony and brotherly affection between all Irishmen.

> 2. The laws enacted by the Parliament established by this Constititution shall, until the achievement of the nation's unity shall otherwise require, have the like area and extent of application as the laws of the Parliament which existed prior to the adoption of this Constitution...[8]

This was a less aggressive, much softer wording than de Valera's and reflected the unity-by-consent approach.

On Article 41.3.2[0], which provides that 'no law shall be enacted providing for the grant of a dissolution of marriage', the Committee also reported unanimously. Besides referring to the validity of the criticism that 'it takes no heed of the wishes of a certain minority of the population who would wish to have divorce facilities', they also pointed out that the Constitution was intended for the whole of Ireland and that 'the prohibition is a source of embarrassment to those seeking to bring about better relations between North and South since the majority of the Northern population have divorce rights under the law applicable to that area.'[9] They suggested that:

> [t]he object underlying this prohibition could be better achieved by using alternative wording which would not give offence to any of the religions professed by the inhabitants of this country. An example of such an alternative would be a provision somewhat on the following lines

>> 'in the case of a person who was married in accordance with the rites of a religion, no law shall be enacted providing for the grant of a dissolution of that marriage on grounds other than those acceptable to that religion.'[10]

On Article 44.1.2[0] (the 'special position' article), they accepted the general view of commentators that the provision had no juridical effect and gave no special privilege to the Catholic Church. Once again looking Northwards, they commented that 'these provisions are ... a useful weapon in the hands of those who are anxious to emphasise the differences between North and South.'[11] They proposed that subsection 2^0 'might profitably be deleted.'[12]

With recommendations like these, the Committee on the Constitution had gone too far and too fast. Their report disappeared almost without trace. Politicians were deeply divided on some of its recommendations, particularly those that were made in the context of the Northern problem. The Fianna Fáil Parliamentary Party by doing nothing disowned their representatives and buried the report. Some, the traditionalists, would not countenance changes in any circumstances: others held that they were not opportune. Nor was the public looking for changes.

That Committee's successor, the Inter-Party Committee on the Implications of Irish Unity, appointed in May 1972, reflected in its title the prevalent view of the time that constitutional amendment was to be viewed primarily in the context of the Northern situation. It was the aspiration to unity that was, as before, to be the engine of change. The Roman Catholic Church, more specifically Cardinal Conway, who was a Northern Ireland man, had taken the lead and declared that the Church would not oppose the deletion of the 'special position' clause in Article 44, thus clearing the way for the amendment enacted in 1972. He had explicitly done so with Northern Ireland in mind: 'if the way to convince our fellow Christians in the North about this is to remove it, then it might be worth the expense of a referendum.'[13] It was now for the politicians to continue with the work of making the house ready for the bride. However, the Inter-Party Committee came rapidly to grief over Articles 2 and 3, and it never reported. By this time, main stream opinion in Fianna Fáil was coming to the view that if there was to be consideration of constitutional amendments to meet the Unionist position, it should only be in the context of an imminent change in the status of the North. Offers of constitutional amendment and legislation would be counters in a bargaining process, to be placed 'on the table' when circumstances warranted. No doubt, it was hinted, Unionists would then find Southern leaders generous. By the middle seventies, this was Fianna Fáil's official position. The predominant view in Fine Gael being that amendment should be proceeded with to allay Northern fears and doubts, thus creating a more favourable climate for negotiations, the question of the timing of changes in the Constitution had become a party political issue. Because of the size of Fianna Fáil support in the country, no

amendment could succeed unless that party backed it. Thus, the
engine of change could not get started.

IV

The leading exponent of the policy of getting on with making the
house ready for the bride was Garret FitzGerald. His influence from
the late sixties to the late eighties was considerable — as an
intellectual upon liberal opinion; as a politician upon Fine Gael;
as Minister for Foreign Affairs and later Taoiseach upon Irish
government policy. The major themes of the nationalist revisionism
of this period can be found systematically argued in his book *Towards
a New Ireland,* first published in 1972.

Firstly, he desired, he said, 'the political reunification of Ireland
achieved with the freely given consent of a majority in Northern
Ireland.'[14] In 1973, he was among the Irish leaders (of the Cosgrave
coalition government) who negotiated the Sunningdale Agreement
which included an Irish government declaration that it 'fully accepted
and solemnly declared that there could no change in the status
of Northern Ireland until a majority of the people of Northern
Ireland desired a change in that status.'

Secondly, he advocated the policy originally put forward in
1967 by the Civil Rights Movement in Northern Ireland — and
later abandoned — of giving priority to internal reforms in the
North itself: 'the first stage of any solution must lie in a reform
of the institutions of government within Northern Ireland.'[15] This
involved pursuing social, civil and political rights in the North itself
in order to better the lot of the nationalist minority. The Irish
government's acceptance at Sunningdale of the principle of unity
only by consent was matched by the acceptance on the part of
the British government that the Republic had some status in Northern
Ireland's affairs for it provided for a 'Council of Ireland' with a
Council of Ministers representing Dublin and the new Belfast
administration, the so-called 'Power-sharing Executive'; a
parliamentary body drawn from the Dáil and the Northern Ireland
Assembly; and a joint secretariat. Henceforward, the British, who
perforce had to continue their direct rule after the Power-sharing
Executive failed in 1973, conceded, though sometimes with
considerable reluctance, that the Irish government could legitimately
press reforms upon it.

Thirdly, FitzGerald contended strongly that any constructive discussion on setting up an all-Ireland state would:

> certainly require concrete evidence on the part of the Republic of a willingness to establish conditions within its own territory that Northern Protestant opinion would find broadly acceptable. ... It seems sensible, therefore, to initiate changes in the Republic in advance of ... a settlement as part of a programme designed to show Northern Protestant opinion that the will to reunification on an acceptable basis is genuine.[16]

Such a programme would include both constitutional changes (in Articles 2, 3, 40, 41 and 44) and amendments to the law relating to censorship, contraception, abortion and the Irish language. The government of the Republic should embark on it as soon as possible. These were the 'more immediate changes required within the Republic to create a favourable atmosphere for future discussions.'[17] Eventually, there would have to be further changes in the Constitution to provide for the establishment of a federal state which was the appropriate form in his view; to safeguard the rights of Northern Protestants in the new Ireland and to spell out a new special relationship between the united Ireland and Great Britain, perhaps including dual citizenship.

There were other sensitivities to be reckoned with besides those of Northern Protestants, and FitzGerald was realistic — though more frank than most — in referring to them. 'The central problem here is the influence of the Catholic Church in the Republic on social and legal issues within the political forum.'[18] He thought that this was not only the matter of the Church's attitude to constitutional and other legal changes but 'much more important to the Northern Protestant is the evidence of indirect influence wielded by the authorities of the Catholic Church.'[19]

The policies proposed by FitzGerald in *Towards a New Ireland* came to be widely accepted in a general way by those who were able to free themselves from the shackles of the traditional nationalist myths. They came to dominate liberal opinion and were strong in Fine Gael and the Labour Party, though not to the total exclusion of more traditional views. In practice, however, the FitzGerald agenda was not taken up: the hostility of Fianna Fáil which, as we have seen had adopted a different strategy, made progress unlikely in any event.

When, a decade after *Towards a New Ireland,* FitzGerald launched his 'constitutional crusade' he was saying much the same things in much the same climate of opinion.In a speech in Seanad Eireann in October 1981 he declared that 'the acid test' of any provision of the Constitution was whether it suited an all-Ireland state. Obviously, he argued, Articles 2 and 3 and some articles that were 'sectarian' or 'confessional' did not pass that test. Moreover, the arguments of those who wished to make no changes until negotiations with the Unionists were under way or in immediate prospect were based upon a 'tragic fallacy'.[20] He questioned whether some in the Republic had yet rid themselves of the partitionist mentality that had informed *Bunreacht na hEireann.* In the next four years the record of the Northern Ireland Forum and the experiences of his coalition government with the referenda on abortion and divorce showed that many had not.

V

The New Ireland Forum, the carefully prepared and elaborately staged conference whose report was published in May 1984, was an initiative taken by 'constitutional nationalists' as they called themselves, from both the Republic and Northern Ireland. It marked a new attempt to reopen the question in an all-Ireland context. A decade of failure since Sunningdale to make progress in resolving Northern problems in a narrow six-county context was, the report said, largely because the problem transcends the context of Northern Ireland.[21] The members of the Forum were setting out to demonstrate that the aspirations of both traditions could be fully accommodated 'in a sovereign, independent Ireland united by agreement.'[22] The hope was that when the blueprint was developed, the British government would thankfully endorse it and cooperate in bringing a new polity into being.

For all the frank analysis and the forthright declaration 'that the civil and religious liberties that they [Northern Protestants] uphold and enjoy will be fully protected and guaranteed and their sense of Britishness accommodated',[23] the Report and, even more, the political wrangling between the parties in the Republic that attended its publication, exposed the limitations of Nationalist thinking. Even the 'positive vision'[24], as the Forum Report put it, of the revisionists did not include a recognition of the basic Unionist claim and the need to come to terms with it. Instead, the authors reiterated the Sunningdale pledge. This envisaged postponing the creation of a new Irish state *until* the Northern majority were wooed. This is to say in effect that the major nationalist objective can be *postponed*, perhaps even indefinitely, but not *abandoned*. Thus the leaders of the nationalist community continued to see their claims as having a moral superiority over those of Unionists. The most deeply held Unionist desire — to remain within a British state and not to be forced to join an Irish one — was eventually, when their local majority had been eroded, to give way to the nationalist objective.

For Northern Unionists the Forum had thus changed nothing. It had served only to underline the danger facing them of being cajoled into an all-Ireland state. The point had been forcefully made at Sunningdale where an agreement was reached between the two sovereign governments in the absence of Unionist representatives and it was being repeated at the New Ireland Forum. It was to be made again at Hillsborough in November, 1985. The Forum Report identified the possible political forms of an all-Ireland state and, because of the need to prevent Fianna Fáil demurring, rank ordered them:

> The particular structure of political unity which the Forum would wish to see established is a unitary state...[25]

The point was rubbed in, and the underlying hard core of traditional national sentiment exposed, by Charles Haughey at his press conference on the Forum as reported in *The Irish Times:*

> Asked what he would say if the Unionists refused to accept a unitary state, Mr Haughey said that in his view nobody was entitled to deny the national unity and unification of this country, and the Forum Report had stated this clearly.[26]

This assumption of moral superiority was further rubbed in — less brutally, though the attitude is no less hard core — by the Bishops' reactions at the Forum to the issue of Northern Protestants' rights. They were in favour of preserving the rights that they currently enjoyed but, as the *Sunday Tribune* put it, 'this was not because of any principled view on their part but a matter of expediency — they were not in favour of according similar religious and civil liberties to Protestants in the South.'[27] Bishop Daly repeated again the 1973 principle:

> We in no way seek to have the moral teaching of the Catholic Church become the criterion of constitutional change ... what we have claimed ... is the right to fulfil our pastoral duty ... to alert the consciences of Catholics to the moral consequences of any proposed piece of legislation. ...[28]

The experience at the referendum in 1983 had demonstrated what that entailed in practice and that experience was to be repeated in 1986. Also, as in the political arena so, too, here the hard-core Catholic view came through at the Forum:

> 'The moral law', 'the common good of all' and 'the objective moral order' ... oblige all, including non-Catholics, because they proceed from right reason ... where the offence to the moral principles of the majority of the citizens would be disproportionately serious it is not unreasonable to require sacrifice of minorities in the interests of the common good.[29]

Thus, in Northern Unionist eyes, not alone did Nationalists, for all their talk of accommodating both traditions, not accord their views equal status, but very little below the surface there persisted hard-core intransigent attitudes. Moreover, those who held them apparently had effective powers of veto. Articles 2 and 3 remained in place and to Unionists Home Rule very evidently continued to be Rome rule.

The vast majority of the people of the Republic regarded Northern Unionists as unreasonably intransigent and believed this to be the root cause of the problem. A liberal-minded revisionist like FitzGerald accepted that there could be no change in the status of Northern Ireland *until* there was agreement. He envisaged a process — admittedly a long one — of changing Unionist minds. This was to be achieved by allaying their fears about the conditions that would obtain inside an all-Ireland state. Obviously he wished, and still believed, it was possible, and many in the Republic adopted this view. Few, though, doubted that theirs was the morally superior position.

Likewise, FitzGerald and many people in the Republic accepted with various degrees of willingness that the change could not come until a majority of the people of the North desired it. FitzGerald made it obvious in his Seanad speech in 1981 that this was a matter not of persuading the majority of Unionists, but of wooing enough of them to join the nationalist minority and support an all-Ireland state. Then, the minority — Protestants — would in the name of democracy have to give way and see their core desire — to remain inside the British state — overridden. The Nationalist belief in the moral superiority of their aim would be boosted by the democratic belief in the right of a majority to prevail. Were this position ever to be reached, little is likely to be heard of one of the most difficult questions in democratic theory, the question of intensity of feelings; whether it is democratic to pursue policies which affront the basic values of a minority and so alienate them.

The moral rights and wrongs of this situation are, however, not going to decide the outcome. Most Nationalists took a long time to grasp one basic feature of the reality of the Northern situation, the existence of two traditions, but many have now accorded the other tradition a measure of legitimacy. What is now needed is for nationalists to recognize and come to terms with the other basic feature of Northern reality, the Unionist veto. Unionists have an effective power of veto. The two sovereign governments either singly or together cannot force them: the record confirms this clearly. The British government could, and might yet, abandon them and withdraw, but that is not likely to achieve the Nationalist objective either. It is more likely to be the occasion of a declaration of an independent state of Ulster.

The appropriate context in which to consider the amendment of *Bunreacht na hEireann* so far as Northern Ireland is concerned is not, therefore, an all-Ireland state of any kind, either now or in the foreseeable future. Increasingly this is becoming recognized in the Republic. Opinion poll evidence published by the Market Research Bureau of Ireland in 1987 suggested that 'the expectation of the country being re-united within the next 10 to 50 years has dropped from 42% in 1983 to 29% ... whilst 60% now see it as unlikely ever to happen or not for at least 100 years.'[30] For purposes of policy making also, the primary objective of Irish politicians in the late eighties, even those of them who continued to proclaim that 'Northern Ireland is a failed political entity', was the urgent need to negotiate and put in place viable regional political institutions in the North and to get representative government and participatory politics going. Both British and Irish governments recognized that this required that they should cooperate and they were cooperating, though sometimes uneasily, within the framework of the Anglo-Irish Agreement. The question for those interested in the development of the Constitution is, then, what if any changes might further this process and help underpin a developing political life in the new Northern Ireland?

It is becoming increasingly obvious — if there was ever any doubt about it — that making changes in the rights provisions of *Bunreacht na hEireann* is irrelevant so far as most Northern Protestants are concerned. Even were they to be made, they would count for very little in the face of the hard line stance of some bishops which was evident at the New Ireland Forum and from statements made during the referenda in 1983 and 1986. Many Northern Protestants believe that, whatever the law, the Church has overwhelming behind-the-scenes influence in the Republic and that it poses a threat to a Protestant community.

What about Articles 2 and 3? Would the formal renunciation of the claims made there make it any more likely that Unionists will accept the *bona fides* of Irish governments when they seek to exert influence upon Northern Ireland affairs or propose functional cooperation in matters of common interest? Perhaps not; but their continued presence in the basic law of the Republic perpetuates a juridical claim which they reject utterly and is a symbol of an intention which they abhor. In FitzGerald's view (in 1981), to remove them 'would by reducing the pressures that gave rise to their [Unionist] siege mentality, open up the possibility of easier dialogue between them and the Nationalists....'[31] While those articles are there, the ability, and perhaps even the will, of British governments to further develop joint policy making will be restricted. Since it is only the British government that can steer the Unionist community towards political structures that have any hope of being accepted by the Nationalist community in the North (which is the objective of the Republic also), it follows that Articles 2 and 3 should be amended.

Since almost any form of words incorporating the traditional nationalist aspiration will evoke the same Unionist reactions as the present articles and since, as we have argued, the aspiration is in any case unachievable, it might be appropriate simply to remove these articles. It does not follow that the Republic has no part to play in the future development of the North. In recent years it has won recognition as a legitimate spokesman and guarantor for the Nationalist community there. Its role in making a contribution to policy formation and its right to question public administration including security have developed over the last decade to an extent unthinkable even a few years before. It is this development that might well offer the best hope for the future of Northern Ireland and the only useful role for the Republic. It is important that it be nurtured and expanded.

VI

If, as seems to be the case, the aspirations of neither Nationalists nor Unionists can be wholly satisfied, practical people should seek, as Charles Carter put it, 'a partial retention by each group of what it considers important'. He argued that it was imperative to provide in perpetuity both for 'the Irish dimension' and 'the non-Irish dimension'. He proposed 'some kind of condominium, that is to say, joint government by Britain and the Republic.'[32]

The concept of condominium is well understood in international law. Introducing it in his *International Law, A Treatise,* Sir Hersch Lauterpacht explains that although 'the supreme authority which a state exercises over its territory would seem to suggest that on one and the same territory there can exist one full sovereign state only', in practice government can and might be divisible:

> The first and perhaps only true exception to that rule is the case of the so-called *condominium.* In this case a piece of territory ... is under the *joint tenancy* of two or more states, these several states exercising sovereignty conjointly over it, and over the individuals living thereon.[33]

In fact, there have been only a few examples and some of these inappropriate to the case of Northern Ireland e.g. involving colonial territories like the Sudan and the New Hebrides. Nevertheless, the possibility of a territory being controlled jointly by two states falls well within the recognized boundaries of international law and political practice.

The idea of an Irish-British condominium in Northern Ireland has from time to time figured among the possibilities canvassed by politicians, academics and journalists. The Social Democratic and Labour Party (SDLP) suggested something of the sort in 1971, but their proposal was for an '*interim* system of government for Northern Ireland under ... joint sovereignty' (author's italics)[34] and was seen as a step towards eventual reunification. It was a notable feature in the New Ireland Forum Report in 1984 where it was presented as one of three options. In contrast to the other two options which incorporated the North into either a unitary all-Ireland state or a federal/confederal all-Ireland state, under this arrangement 'the London and Dublin governments would have equal responsibility for all aspects of the government of Northern Ireland.' They would establish 'a joint authority' which 'would give political, symbolic and administrative expression of their identity to Northern nationalists without infringing the parallel wish of unionists to maintain and to have full operational expression of their identity.' Although this shared rule 'could be exercised directly, there would be enabling provision for the exercise of major powers by a locally-elected Assembly and Executive.' The Report envisaged automatic joint citizenship and an 'enforceable non-denominational Bill of Rights.'[35] The report of the sub-committee which prepared this proposal for consideration contained further details e.g. both flags would·be used and would be flown together; there would be a new police service; there would be a 'Constitutional Court' to interpret and enforce the Treaty or binding agreement under which the condominium was created.[36] (However, sterling would remain the local currency of Northern Ireland!) With a joint authority arrangement such as this:

> the two traditions in Northern Ireland would find themselves on a basis of equality and both would be able to find an expression of their identity in the new institutions. There would be no diminution of the Britishness of the Unionist population. Their identity, ethos and link with Britain would be assured by the authority and presence of the British government in the joint authority arrangements. At the same time it would resolve... the failure to give satisfactory political, symbolic and administrative expression to Northern nationalists.[37]

Whenever it had been raised, the idea of a condominium or something like it tended inevitably to be pushed to one side by the protagonists of both communities in their futile pursuit of unattainable objectives. A like fate befell it with a vengeance on this occasion. The proposal was immediately rejected by Haughey in his uncompromising stand on the unitary all-Ireland state option, which was indeed, as he contended, the explicitly preferred solution offered in the Report. In practice, however, once the British government accepted that the Irish government had a role in Northern Ireland and British-Irish consultation and cooperation got underway in an organized fashion, the first steps down the road that could lead to condominium had in fact been taken.

Movement in this direction has been hesitant and pragmatic. The institutions and procedures that have evolved are not set in any context of a constitutional framework or agreed formulae. Cooperation in policy development and the surveillance of security operations, judicial processes and other aspects of public administration has grown, however, and might well continue to grow organically. It might be nurtured in some areas the more quickly by the advent of the single European market, the increasing emphasis on harmonization in the European Economic Community and the growing opportunities for joint economic ventures between North and South. Nevertheless, there was no question in the late eighties about which government rules Northern Ireland. Any talk of 'joint authority' at best lay well in the future. It would, in any event, have to be preceded by the development of participatory politics in the North involving both communities. Northern Ireland is not an underdeveloped territory like the Sudan or the New Hebrides to be ruled by two imperial powers. It needs, and its people in both communities desire, considerable powers of self-government devolved upon it. It is the policy of both governments to promote this. It is just possible that eventually Northern Ireland could be ruled by consensus within a framework of tripartite institutions. It is hard to see that it could be ruled on a popular basis in any other way. The onus lies upon the politicians of the Republic as well as the British government to seek to maximize the chances of developing such popular provincial government. Without it, the tripartite institutions will never evolve. It is in this light that the question of changes in *Bunreacht na hEireann* having regard to Northern Ireland ought to be considered.

— 8 —

The European Communities and the Constitution

IRELAND'S ACCESSION TO the European Communities in January 1973 brought the state into 'a new type of international organization with much greater powers over member countries than those traditionally given to international institutions.'[1] Membership of the Communities — the European Coal and Steel Community (the Treaty of Paris, 1951), the European Economic Community (the Treaty of Rome, 1957) and the European Atomic Energy Community (the Treaty of Rome, 1957) — imposes obligations and confers rights not only in the Treaties themselves but also by virtue of what the members have wished upon themselves through the various organs of the Communities since they came together.

A potent source of law such as the Communities are could hardly fail to have an impact upon Irish law, including constitutional law. When Ireland joined, it came into a polity which already had fifteen years of rule making behind it. The law of the Communities, both the Treaties and this body of secondary legislation, had to be received into Irish law and, in addition, there had perforce to be an open door through which future Community law could be received. These were the obligations of membership but they could not legally be undertaken under the Constitution as it then stood. A constitutional amendment (the Third Amendment of the Constitution Act, 1972) was needed before Ireland could join: another (the Tenth Amendment of the Constitution Act) was required in 1987 before the government could ratify the Single European Act that formalized the developing practices and institutions of political cooperation that had evolved over the years. By the the end of the eighties, with the Community institutions straining to accomplish the major objective of a truly common internal market by 1 January 1993 — the year that will mark twenty years of Irish membership — the potential effects of belonging to an institution which can create rights and obligations as the Communities can were almost incalculable. A British judge, Lord Justice Denning, aptly described the impact of Community law as 'like an incoming tide. It flows into the estuaries and up the rivers. It cannot be held back.'[2] *Bunreacht na hEireann* itself and Irish constitutional law are being washed by this tide and will increasingly be as time passes.

II

Unlike Ireland, Community members such as France, Germany and Italy which had made fresh starts after the second world war reflected in their new post-war constitutions the strong disposition of continental western European political leaders to qualify the concept of sovereignty. Reviewing them, Carl J. Friedrich thought that 'perhaps the most novel aspect of these constitutions is their abandonment of national sovereignty as a central presupposition of their political theory.'[3] In such a political climate and with appropriately conceived basic law, it was not difficult for these countries to accommodate to membership of the European Communities. Ireland, by contrast, had a pre-war constitution and unlike the states of continental western Europe had enjoyed unbroken political stability since its inception. It is not surprising that *Bunreacht na hEireann,* framed as it was in the middle thirties, did not fit Ireland to enter a political organization like the Communities, for it belonged to an era that did not contemplate such a political entity. The Constitution reflected the 'dualist' approach to the relationship between international law and domestic law. The basic principle of the dualist approach is that there are two separate and quite distinct legal systems: one regulates relations between states; the other between persons in a state. They are different in subject matter and content.

Article 29.6 of the Constitution 'explicitly lays down a "dualist" approach to international law.'[4] It requires that the state shall determine for itself how and to what extent it will receive international law:

> No international agreement shall be part of the domestic law
> of the State save as may be determined by the Oireachtas.

During the late sixties, when Ireland was an applicant for
membership of the Communities, the constitutional difficulties
involved were teased out by lawyers and civil servants. One of those
involved, John Temple Lang, summed them up in this way:

> Since the Community Treaties must be received into Irish law
> by an Act of the Irish legislature, the provisions of the Treaties
> cannot become part of Irish law unless they are consistent
> with the provisions of the Irish Constitution. As it is at present
> the Irish Constitution does not allow the legislature to confer
> on the Community institutions the powers which belong to
> them under the Treaties, so as to make these powers effective
> under Irish law. [5]

'The powers which belong to them under the Treaties': these are
the significant words. Article 29.6 is appropriate for situations in
which the state assumes ordinary treaty obligations, including treaties
that purport to create human rights. Such treaties might impose
an obligation upon a country to alter its domestic law, but
appropriate action is entirely a matter for the government and
parliament of that country. They might also include arrangements
by which states bind themselves in advance to accept the jurisdiction
of judicial institutions and even to allow individual citizens to proceed
against states, as the European Convention on Human Rights does,
but these too are matters entirely for the states to decide for
themselves. Those who signed the Treaties of Rome and Paris,
however, were doing much more than this. Those Treaties created
'a new legal order of international law for the benefit of which
the [member] States have limited their sovereign rights, albeit within
limited fields, and the subjects of which comprise not only member
states but also their nationals.'[6]

A government White Paper in 1970 listed a number of provisions
of the Constitution that would 'have to be considered' were Ireland
to decide to join and noted provisions of the EEC Treaty that 'could
be held to be inconsistent with' or 'in conflict with' the Constitution. [7]
It was also recognized that some domestic ordinary legislation would
have to be amended. Instead of making a whole series of changes
in the Constitution, which would have been a complicated business,
it was decided to insert a single enabling section into the Constitution
that would permit Ireland to join and would provide that no

legislation or actions needed to give effect to Community measures could be invalidated by reason of unconstitutionality. Accordingly, the Third Amendment of the Constitution Act, agreed in a referendum in May 1972, added one sub-section to Article 29.4. as follows:

> 3^0 The State may become a member of the European Coal and Steel Community (established by Treaty signed at Paris on the 18th day of April, 1951), the European Economic Community (established by Treaty signed at Rome on the 25th day of March, 1957) and the European Atomic Energy Community (established by Treaty signed at Rome on the 15th day of March, 1957). No provision of this Constitution invalidates laws enacted, acts done or measures adopted by the State necessitated by the obligations of membership of the Communities or prevents laws enacted, acts done or measures adopted by the Communities, or institutions thereof, from having the force of law in the State.

This, it was held, would allow the state to honour its obligations while obviating the need to make a whole series of changes, some of which would have presented difficulty. The way was thus cleared for an accession act, the European Communities Act, 1972 (no. 27), which completed the process. Section 2 of that act provided that from 1 January 1973:

> the treaties governing the European Communities and the existing and future acts adopted by the institutions of those Communities shall be binding on the state and shall be part of the domestic law thereof under the conditions laid down in those treaties.

Section 3 (i) provided that 'a Minister of State may make regulations for enabling Section 2 of this Act to have full effect.'

The same procedure was necessary in 1987, when a major extension of the Communities' range of activities and measures to strengthen Community institutions — lumped together and misleadingly entitled the Single European Act — came up for ratification by the member states. Following a Supreme Court decision (in *Crotty* v. *An Taoiseach* [1987] I.L.R.M. 400) that ratification of part of that act would require a constitutional amendment, the Tenth Amendment of the Constitution Act, 1987 was approved by referendum to allow Ireland to fulfil its Community obligations. It took the form of an addition to Article 29.4. 3^0 (the subsection inserted in 1972):

> The State may ratify the Single European Act signed on behalf
> of the Member States of the Communities at Luxembourg
> on the 17th day of February, 1986 and at the Hague on the
> 28th day of February 1986.

III

The wording of Article 29.4.3^0 as amended in 1987 and the provisions
of the European Communities Act, 1972 provide the legal conduit
through which Community law flows into Irish law. However, there
is more to the relationship than this. The status of Community
law was from the beginning consistently enhanced by decisions of
the Communities' judicial arm, the Court of Justice. An American
constitutional lawyer, Frank Casper, described the process as
follows:

> Starting with the need of assuring the uniformity of Community
> law throughout the member nations, the Court of Justice has
> transformed the treaties underlying the European Commun-
> ity... into the Constitution of the Community.[8]

It can truly be said that 'Ireland has two Constitutions now.'[9]

What is more, this 'off-shore' Constitution, as it has been called,
in its own sphere predominates over *Bunreacht na hEireann*, the
domestic Constitution. This superiority, first authoritatively
enunciated by the European Court in the case of *Costa* v. *E.N.E.L.*
(case 6164 [1964] C.M.L.R. 425) as early as 1964 and reiterated
and expanded again and again since, was well summarised by Jacques
Delors, the President of the Commission, in an answer to a question
in the European Parliament:

> It is clear from the wording of the Treaties and from repeated
> decisions of the Court of Justice of the European Communities
> that the Community legislation in force takes precedence over
> national provisions, whatever their nature. Rules contained
> in the national constitutions are no exception... As regards
> the application of existing Community law, it makes no
> appreciable difference whether procedures for monitoring the
> constitutionality of laws exist in a Member State or not.[10]

The precedence of Community law in its own sphere was from
the beginning clearly acknowledged in Irish law. As we have seen

(see above pp. 98-99), the drafters of the Third Amendment had obviously, in Michael Forde's words, 'determined that, because of the Constitution's "dualistic" nature, it should be stipulated quite plainly that E.E.C. law takes precedence over domestic law and indeed over the Constitution itself.'[11] The effect of the Third Amendment, as of the Tenth also, is that Community law is insulated from constitutional challenge. This 'constitution-proofing' applies to Community Regulations and Directives, to the laws made by the Oireachtas required by these measures and to instruments made under the European Communities Act, 1972 insofar as they are 'necessitated by the obligations of membership'. Other matters are subject to judicial scrutiny, but, as Chief Justice Finlay put it in the case of *Crotty* v. *An Taoiseach,* where such questions of constitutionality do arise, the decisions of the European Court 'on the interpretation of the Treaty and on questions covering its implementation take precedence, in case of conflict, over the domestic law and the decision of national courts of Member States.'[12]

This body of binding law is of two kinds, Community legislative instruments and court rulings. Legislation takes a number of forms. Some of it will not have been passed by the Oireachtas: it has the force of law when made by the appropriate Community institution. For the rest, member governments are bound to take steps to implement it. Article 189 of the Treaty of Rome establishing the European Economic Community is quite explicit about this:

> In order to carry out their task the Council and the Commission shall, in accordance with the provisions of this Treaty, make regulations, issue directives, take decisions, make recommendations or deliver opinions.
> A regulation shall have general application. It shall be binding in its entirety and directly applicable in all Member States.
> A directive shall be binding, as to the result to be achieved, upon each Member State to which it is addressed, but shall leave to the national authorities the choice of form and methods.
> A decision shall be binding in its entirety upon those to whom it is addressed.

Even in respect of a directive, where the national authorities have 'the choice of form and methods', they are little more than subordinate agents of Brussels whom they must satisfy. Nor can they delay too long about it. In answer to the question posed by an Italian court: 'Does Council Directive 73/173/EEC of 4 June

1973... constitute directly applicable legislation conferring upon individuals personal rights which the national courts must protect?', the Court of Justice ruled that:

> a Member State which has not adopted the implementing measures required by the directive in the prescribed periods may not rely, as against individuals, on its own failure to perform the obligations which the directive entails.... It follows that a national court requested by a person who has complied with the provisions of a directive not to apply a national provision incompatible with the directive not incorporated into the internal legal order of a defaulting Member State, must uphold that request if the obligation in question is unconditional and sufficiently precise.[13]

Clearly, the Oireachtas is now very far from having in practice what the Constitution still in one place (Article 15) says it has, namely 'the sole and exclusive power of making laws for the State'. Through its Joint Committee (i.e. composed of members of both the Dáil and the Seanad) on the Secondary Legislation of the European Communities it has some opportunity to take note of and comment on proposals made by the Commission to the Council of Ministers for legislation (regulations, directives etc.), on acts of Community institutions and on Irish statutory instruments, i.e. ministerial regulations implementing Community legislation. With the increase in the power and virility of the European Parliament, it is rather the Irish MEPs who are better placed than members of the Oireachtas to exert what influence can be applied by parliamentarians to community law making. Of course, the more important influence is that which ministers and senior civil servants can exert upon formulators of policy, the Commission and the Council of Ministers. From its early days the Joint Committee was at least effective in checking the propensity of some government departments to exploit their rule-making power under the European Communities Act, 1972. However, its reports usually attract little attention. Likewise, the twice yearly *Report on Developments in the European Communities,* which by law the government must present to the Oireachtas, is rarely debated.

As with the legislature, so too with the judiciary. Article 34.1 of the Constitution provides that 'justice shall be administered in courts established by law by judges appointed in the manner provided by this Constitution....' Further, under Article 34.4.6^0, the decision

of the Supreme Court is 'in all cases ... final and conclusive.'
However, the Court of Justice of the European Communities (the
European Court) which has the function under the Treaties of
ensuring that Community law is observed, stands alongside and
in certain circumstances above, the Irish courts. Article 177 of the
Treaty of Rome provides that where any question involving the
validity and interpretation of Community laws or measures is raised
in a case before a domestic court ,that court may refer, and if it
is a final court of appeal, must refer the matter to the European
Court. That court cannot intervene directly in cases before domestic
courts, but there is a procedure by which 'preliminary rulings', as
Article 177 puts it, can be sought, thus giving the European Court
the opportunity to interpret points of Community law involved.[14]
The domestic court or tribunal (for the procedure has been opened
up to bodies such as the Labour Court) is obliged to apply the
rulings given in deciding the case. When there is a conflict of laws
the view of the European Court prevails as the quotation from
Chief Justice Finlay (see above p. 101) makes clear. Where, as has
occurred in Italy, for example, domestic courts have attempted to
take a different view, the European Court has reacted vigorously
and asserted the supremacy of Community law. In appropriate
circumstances where the Commission considers that a member state
has failed to fulfil its Treaty obligations, it has the power under
Article 169 of the EEC Treaty to take proceedings against it in
the European Court. In the first decade of its membership Ireland
was so arraigned in five cases and in all of them it was held to
have been in breach. All in all, there seems little doubt that Ireland,
like all the member states, is locked irrevocably into a legal and
constitutional system that over a considerable area of state activity
is Community dominated.

This is not the only major change in the nature of the Irish
legal system consequent upon Community membership. It is a feature
of the Communities that the subjects of this powerful new legal
order comprise not only member states, as would be the case in
international law, but their nationals as well. Community institutions
have the power to legislate directly for individuals and other legal
persons e.g. companies, imposing duties and conferring rights upon
them. Traditionally, states had been slow to allow their citizens
to bring them before international courts: under the legal system
of the Communities, the rights and duties that are created within

the system can be enforced against any aggrieved citizens' own public authorities through the courts, both domestic and in Luxembourg.

IV

This direct relationship between the citizens (and other legal persons) of the member states and the Community regime is the more significant because of its implications for the evolution and enforcement of human rights. In this area, too, the European Court has been increasingly active and assertive over the years. Although the European Economic Community Treaty, which is the one that matters most in this respect, does not contain a section on fundamental rights as do most state constitutions, some of its provisions are clearly statements of rights. For example, Article 7 prohibits discrimination on grounds of nationality 'within the scope of application of this Treaty'; Article 48 provides for freedom of movement within the Community; Article 119 enunciates the principle of equal pay for equal work. Others have been identified by the European Court over the years as in effect implying general principles of law that create rights for individuals, for example, the right to be heard in one's defence.[15] By the early seventies the Court had gone further and identified two potentially very fertile sources of rights outside what had hitherto been regarded as Community law, namely, the constitutions of member states and the European Convention for the Protection of Human Rights and Fundamental Freedoms (1950).[16] The Court's stance was endorsed on 5 April 1977 when a 'Joint Declaration' by the European Parliament, the Council and the Commission proclaimed that:

1. The European Parliament, the Council and the Commission stress the prime importance they attach to the protection of fundamental rights, as derived in particular from the constitutions of the Member States and the European Convention for the Protection of Human Rights and Fundamental Freedoms.
2. In the exercise of their powers and in pursuance of the aims of the European Communities they respect and will continue to respect these rights.

Subsequently, mention was made of these as sources of rights in the Preamble to the Single European Act.

The recognition at Community level of the European Convention on Human Rights was particularly important for Irish people. Ireland had signed the convention a quarter of a century before, thus accepting an obligation in international law, but nothing was subsequently done systematically to enact into domestic law those rights which it enunciated that were not already there. By 1983, however, John Temple Lang could say that, as a result of the European Court's activities:

> at least in the sphere of directly applicable community law, the provisions of the Convention are, in effect, now a part of Irish law. The European Convention can now be relied on in the Irish courts in the Community sphere, almost as if it had been enacted into Irish law.[17]

Generally, the rights affected by Community action are not the classic liberal rights such as belief, conscience or freedom from arrest: rather it is economic and social rights that have been identified, expanded and enforced. Among the most important have been the outlawing of discrimination on the grounds of nationality; equality between the sexes in respect of pay, access to employment, training and promotion; the right to set up in business, practise a profession or go to work anywhere in the Community; protection for migrant workers; competition and discrimination in business. The trend towards identifying basic principles of law, together with the recognition of the rights in the constitutions of the member states and the introduction of the European Convention on Human Rights as potential sources of law mark a wider interest in human rights by the Court of Justice and Community institutions generally. It is in this area that great developments might be anticipated in the future which will have an important impact on Ireland.

V

It will have become obvious that the law-making power of the Community institutions, both legislative and judicial, are considerable and have enormous implications for Irish law and government. These are, however, impossible to specify exhaustively for *there are no set limits to Community power*. The relationship between the two polities, the Community regime and the member state, by no means conforms to the federal principle, where the functions, competence and powers of each party are specified. Writing about the European Economic Community Treaty, John Temple Lang stated that:

> it is what is called a 'framework-treaty' (traité-cadre) which, instead of merely laying down rules, also provides institutions and machinery by which new legal measures may be adopted and differences of opinion resolved.[18]

So, too, are the other treaties establishing the Coal and Steel and Atomic Energy Communities. In this respect they are like constitutions; they have the capacity for development. As we have seen, they, and particularly the EEC Treaty, are indeed very well endowed to push out the frontiers of their own competence, if the members so wish. It is the same in the cse of the Single European Act. As John Temple Lang put it:

> the boundary between exclusive Community powers and national powers is a moving boundary. Since the Single Act, there are now no clear legal limits (no doubt there are political ones) on how far it may move.[19]

Under the Treaties, Community institutions have exclusive powers to deal with some subjects. For example, under the E.E.C. Treaty commercial policy and the control of sea fishing policy are reserved to the Community. Likewise, the Coal and Steel and the Atomic Energy Treaties give exclusive powers. However, powers derived from explicit statements in the Treaties by no means exhaust the sphere of exclusive competence. The Communities can and do acquire exclusive competence not only from the Treaties directly but from secondary legislation. The effect of this is that 'the boundary between exclusive Community powers and national powers is a moving boundary.'[20] Significantly the movement so far has been in one direction only, in favour of the Communities, and this is likely to continue. John Temple Lang again:

> The areas in which national measures are prohibited... will widen gradually over time, as the number and scope of Community measures increase.[21]

The propensity of the Economic Community in particular to extend its power and to encroach upon the competence of the member states is the further increased by the potential offered in Article

5. This article is a statement in the most general terms of the obligations of members:

> Member states shall take all appropriate measures, whether general or particular, to ensure fulfilment of the obligations arising out of this Treaty or resulting from action taken by the institutions of the Community. They shall facilitiate the achievement of the Community's tasks.
> They shall abstain from any measure which could jeopardise the attainment of the objectives of this Treaty.

Already it has offered considerable scope for the European Court that has shown itself to be more than willing to push out the frontiers. In the view of John Temple Lang 'its implications extend much further than is generally realized.'[22] He suggests that these include obligations as yet not spelled out with any precision, to give full effect to Community objectives; to enforce Community law; not to interfere with the operation of Community law, rules or institutions; to cooperate with other member states and to join them in collective action; to consult the Commission and keep it informed. If this is the case — the Court certainly seems from the trend of its rulings to be moving in this direction — Article 5 is the basis of a whole range of legal principles which will fundamentally alter the traditional picture of what statehood implies and what *Bunreacht na hEireann* appears to say.

VI

The organic nature of the European Communities and the consequential encroachment into areas formerly under the jurisdiction of member states only slowly came to be recognized by Irish people generally until, after a decade of relative stagnation from the middle seventies until the middle eighties, a sudden leap forward produced the Single European Act (SEA). This was the product of 'the creative initiative of Jacques Delors and of the new European Commission of which he became President ... which was to make profound changes in the European landscape and ... in the Community's methods of work.'[23]

In Ireland (as also in Denmark) a constitutional referendum was required before the SEA could be ratified. The debate engendered by the legal challenge of Dr Raymond Crotty and the cases in the High Court and the Supreme Court in which his view that ratification required a constitutional amendment was upheld, together with the subsequent referendum, did more to inform and educate Irish people about the implications of Community membership than had the previous fourteen years experience of it.

The SEA 'contains important innovations, which might lead to significant changes in the behaviour of the institutions and in the way in which the Community itself will develop.'[24] It is 'Single' only in the sense that it is one instrument. In fact, it contains two collections of measures, both designed to bring about great changes. The first (in Title II) comprises amendments to the Treaties themselves, altering the functions and powers of Community organs, making arrangements to complete the internal market by the end of 1992, providing for the reduction of regional disparities and extending the competence of the Community, e.g. to the health and safety of workers, to the protection of the environment and to technological development. The second (Title III) seeks to consolidate the progress made towards political cooperation by formalizing the practices and institutions that had grown up over the years and thus to enhance their status and develop them. Michael Forde summarised it as follows:

> What Title III seeks to do is to place such co-operation on a formal basis by having the methods and scope of co-operation spelled out in a binding treaty and by giving the entire enterprise a quasi-institutional embodiment under the name European Political Cooperation.[25]

As he points out, it is in reality a treaty, although not so in name: it supplements the founding Treaties of Rome and Paris. The practice of member states consulting on foreign policy issues was now raised to the status of a binding obligation. Henceforth, each member state would be required to consult and to take account of the views of other members before deciding its policy. However, it would not be bound by Community law to follow a common policy and the Treaty provisions in respect of the powers of the Court of Justice specifically do not cover Title III.

When the Irish government moved to ratify the Single European Act by seeking, first, to get the Oireachtas to enact the European Communities Bill, 1986, to cover Title II and , second, to get the

Dáil to pass a resolution approving of Title III as if it were a treaty, as required by Article 29.5 of the Constitution, Dr Raymond Crotty, a leading opponent of Ireland's membership of the Communities, sought an order from the Irish courts preventing the government from depositing the instrument of ratification on the grounds that it would be unconstitutional. The Crotty case is of great constitutional significance both for what it settled and what it left uncertain.

The Court was concerned with two main issues — there were others also. The first was the constitutionality of the European Communities Act, 1986, which purported to bring Title II and some other provisions of the SEA into the domestic law of the state by amending the original European Communities Act of 1972. The question was whether or not any amendment of the Treaties required a further amendment of *Bunreacht na hEireann* as Crotty contended. The Supreme Court decided that:

> the first sentence in Article 29(4) 3^0 of the Constitution must be construed as an authorisation given to the State not only to join the Communities as they stood in 1973 , but also to join in amendments of the Treaties so long as such amendments do not alter the essential scope or objectives of the Communities.
> To hold that the first sentence of Article 29(4) 3^0 does not authorise any form of amendment to the Treaties after 1973 without further amendment of the Constitution would be too narrow a construction; to construe it as an open ended authority to agree, without further amendment of the Constitution, to any amendment of the Treaties would be too broad. [26]

It was, then, for the Court to examine the amendments. Having done so it decided that they fell within the scope of Article $29.4.3^0$:

> The Community was ... a developing organism with diverse and changing methods for making decisions and an inbuilt and clearly expressed objective of expansion and progress. ...

The second main issue in this case was whether it was unconstitutional for the government to ratify a treaty which would oblige future governments, as the Chief Justice put it:

> to consult; to take full account of the position of other partners, to ensure that common principles and objectives are gradually

developed and defined; as far as possible to refrain from impeding the formation of a consensus and the joint action which this would produce; to be ready to cooperate policies more closely on the political aspects of security.[27]

On this issue the Court was divided. The decision by three to two was that the ratification of Title III of the SEA would require an appropriate constitutional amendment. Clearly the majority believed, as Michael Forde put it, 'that Title III of the SEA involved a drastic transformation in the nature of the European Communities, rendering them no longer an essentially economic union and instead crossing the threshold of a political community within which Ireland's foreign policy would be no longer guided as previously by the national interest.'[28]

The decision in the *Crotty* case led to some criticism of the judiciary — more accurately of some judges. Mostly, it was the conservative nature of the majority decision and the implications for executive-judiciary relationships of some statements made in the course of the judgements that evoked comment from both politicians and some members of the legal profession. In particular, the Dáil debate on the bill to amend the Constitution made necessary by the judgement was the occasion for — metaphorically speaking — raised eyebrows all round and in some cases overt criticism.[29] The Taoiseach (C. J. Haughey) said that the judgements had caused 'widespread surprise'.[30] Garret FitzGerald, his predecessor now in opposition, had already described the decision as 'extraordinary' and both he and his former Minister for Foreign Affairs, Peter Barry, openly disagreed with it.[31] The embarrassment which the ruling had caused them and their colleagues in the previous coalition government perhaps partly explains their criticism. They had accepted legal advice that ratification would not require a constitutional referendum and from the autumn of 1986 they had pooh-poohed the views of those who suggested that it would, or it might, or that, in any case in matters of this sort, the approval of the people would be desirable. Some lawyers were also surprised and a few critical, though discreetly so. Distinguished Community law specialists like Senator Mary Robinson SC and Dr John Temple Lang (at that time in the Legal Service of the Commission) had given their opinion before the case that ratification would not necessitate an amendment. In Temple Lang's words: 'there does not seem to be any reason for saying that the Single Act is unconstitutional, or that it makes a new referendum necessary.'[32]

Besides the public criticism of the legal arguments there was a political dispute between those, like the members of the coalition government and indeed the great majority of active politicians, who claimed that Ireland had everything to gain from embracing this Delors initiative, and a small but vocal anti-Community group. They not only argued that many Community policies were bad for Irish people but also raised emotive issues like the implications of European political cooperation for Irish neutrality and, more generally, the erosion of sovereignty. These were political hot potatoes and most politicians of all the major parties would have preferred that they were not produced.

Although the *Crotty* case resolved the question of the Government's competence in respect of one foreign policy issue, it unfortunately raised important general questions about the extent of its powers in this area. Doubts were voiced on two scores. The first concerned the extent of the courts' powers to review the Government's foreign policy decisions. Some saw the result, in the words of one legal authority, as 'a judicial rap on the executive knuckles.'[33] However, in delivering their judgements the judges seemed to express a range of views about the role of the courts in upholding the Constitution by restraining governments, an issue previously raised in the case of *Boland* v. *An Taoiseach* ([1974] I.R. 338). The second concerned, as Michael Forde put it, 'the extent to which the State may become a party to international institutional arrangements whereby its freedom to deal with other states becomes extensively circumscribed'.[34] The doubts that were raised on this score, if valid, are very serious indeed.

The *Crotty* case in the view of some authorities has not only posed major problems for the conduct of foreign policy but has also cast doubt on some existing treaty commitments. Finbarr Murphy, an expert in this field of law, put it thus:

> The really serious implication of the Crotty judgement concerns the status and validity of certain international commitments entered into by the State. In short, wherever the State is involved in an international arrangement which stipulates that a particular procedure for consultation and discussion should be followed, then the limitations on the exercise of the State's foreign policy inherent in that arrangement are inconsistent with the Constitution. . . by far the most obvious international agreement at risk under the Crotty doctrine is the Anglo-Irish Agreement of 1985.[35]

As he pointed out, that agreement required the parties to seek to resolve political, legal and security issues by agreement and to pursue cooperative policies in cross-border matters: it also provided for institutions and procedures, notably the Intergovernmental Conference and Secretariat, to that end. The similarities with what was in Title III of the SEA were obvious. Murphy urged that 'consideration should be given to framing a wider amendment which would — if approved — secure the ratification of the SEA and protect the state's other international obligations at the same time.'[36]

In choosing the form of words it did for the enabling amendment, the government adopted what might be called a 'minimalist' solution and deliberately did not address these problems. The amendments of Article 29 are extremely cautious and not very European-minded. That was perhaps inevitable at the time for, with the other member states waiting upon Ireland, it was necessary to decide on the form of the Tenth Amendment and to get it enacted without delay. However, one of the consequences of pursuing this policy was that it left unresolved the doubts about the government's competence to conduct foreign affairs.

VII

The method which the government of the day chose in order to enable Ireland to join the Communities, namely the insertion of an enabling sub-section in Article 29, was no doubt in the short term neat, simple and convenient. Experience apparently suggested that it had caused no practical difficulties for governments, since the same formula was used in 1987 in order to permit Ireland to ratify the SEA. However, the result of proceeding in this manner is that the Constitution contains statements that are negatived elsewhere in the document. Reference has already been made to some of these in this chapter e.g. the Oireachtas clearly does not have 'the sole and exclusive power of making laws for the State' nor is justice administered only by courts 'appointed in the manner provided by this Constitution.' Again, some articles of the Treaties and the SEA. and some actions of Community legislative and judicial organs have created rights and imposed duties that perhaps ought to be mentioned in the rights section of the Constitution by way of amendments that add to or alter what is at present there.

The experience of ratifying the SEA and the doubts that have arisen about the possible implications of the *Crotty* case point in the same direction. This was recognized and remarked upon by some politicians at the time. Arguing that the proposed constitutional amendment ought to have been more widely drawn than it was, Deputy Desmond O'Malley, leader of the Progressive Democrats, pointed to the need to head off the problems that might arise:

> Some of the judgements in Crotty's case should also cause us to ponder on our own constitutional division of powers. Do these need amendment or do they need restatement or re-assertion? Are some of the judgements seeking to amend the division of powers by purporting to give the courts a function in policy making or in policy review?[37]

Criticizing the view put forward by Mr Justice Henchy in his judgement in the *Crotty* case, O'Malley commented that 'if he [Henchy] is right in his interpretation of our Constitution, we need not just a broad amendment now — we may well need a new Constitution.' Others including the leader of the Labour Party, Dick Spring, like O'Malley a lawyer also, took the same view. Garret FitzGerald, the former Taoiseach, argued that it was clearly the intention of the Constitution to give the government wide powers to develop the country's foreign relations and in support of this he quoted that best of authorities, Eamon de Valera:

> The idea of this Constitution is to put this matter of our external relations in its proper position relatively to the Constitution, and that is outside it, as a matter of foreign policy, to be determined from time to time, according as the people's interests suggest to them that they should put this government or that government into office with powers to implement their will. That is what is done here.[38]

If, FitzGerald argued, the letter of the Constitution had 'let us down in some curious way', it was essential 'to take the necessary action.'[39]

It is obvious that the European dimension in Irish politics makes a revision of the Constitution both necessary and urgent, if only for the sake of coherence. It would be foolish, however, to imagine that this process could ever be a simple matter of harmonization and clarification let alone a 'once-off' process of *aggiornamento*. The Communities are in process of constant organic growth, sometimes as at the end of the eighties, rapid growth. It was the intention of the founders 'to lay the foundations of an ever-closer union among the peoples of Europe,' as the preamble to the Treaty of Rome puts it, and engines of change were provided to do this. As this chapter has attempted to show, the very nature of the Treaties (their *traité cadre* aspect), the implications of Article 5, the expansionist demeanour of the Court of Justice, and, perhaps most important, the implications of the Single European Act all bear witness to this. It must be expected , therefore, that the process of constitutional harmonization will need to be repeated from time to time. The first revision is now overdue.

To take up this task would certainly pose considerable problems for any Irish government. The shibboleths associated with the concept of neutrality Irish-style and the inhibitions against becoming involved in European defence policy issues, though based on dubious premises, are nevertheless widely held and thus facts of political life of which governments must take account. So, too, is the more abstract concept of 'sovereignty'. Especially when it has prefixed to it the adjective 'national' it still has political force.

During the debates preceding the referendum on joining the Communities, much was made of the danger to Irish sovereignty. By joining, it was argued, Ireland would lose her sovereignty or some part of it. The argument was strongly put once again by the opponents of the SEA, a small but intellectually able and persistent opposition. The *Crotty* case was the outcome of their activities: the Supreme Court decision was a vindication of some at least of their arguments. From a constitutional point of view, accession to a political organization as powerful as the European Communities might, indeed, seem to put in question the wording of Article 5 which declares that 'Ireland is a sovereign, independent, democratic state.'

'Sovereignty', which is defined in a government White Paper about the implications of joining the Communities as 'autonomous powers of decision over domestic and foreign policies', is a very slippery concept, as much political as legal. As the government saw it then (1970):

> all international cooperation involves some limitation on sovereignty. Even a simple bilateral trade agreement with its reciprocal commitments, places curbs on the freedom of action of the parties. International agreements to which Ireland is a party, such as the General Agreement on Tariffs and Trade,

the Statute of the Council of Europe, the European Convention on Human Rights or the Charter of the United Nations, place obligations on the participating states, some of which involve substantial derogations from sovereignty.[40]

It can, of course, be argued that at some point in the process of undertaking such obligations and ceding powers of decision to international bodies, the term sovereign becomes inappropriate. European law has for twenty years been explicit in recognizing the limitations upon state sovereignty imposed by membership: 'the grant made by the member states to the Community of rights and powers in accordance with the provisions of the Treaty involves a definitive limitation on their sovereign rights to override this limitation.'[41] In any case, the scope of Community action is wider than, and the nature of the Communities different from, other international cooperative arrangements.

What is more, two of the three Treaties have no time limits: they are 'concluded for an unlimited period' (Treaty of Rome, Article 240). The other, the European Coal and Steel Community Treaty, runs for fifty years. In no case is there a unilateral right of withdrawal. Were a state to denounce them, the European Court would probably hold parties in the denouncing state to be bound in law. More important, they are now bound almost if not completely irrevocably by the facts of economic, social and political life.

Wide though the scope of, and broad, the powers of the Communities are, they are not unrestricted. Membership involves, in particular, no military or defence commitments. Nevertheless as political cooperation developed so inevitably these matters began to creep onto the agendas of ministerial meetings. By 1975, the Commission, which has often tended to go ahead of the member states in these matters, was outlining the indispensable conditions of what by that time was already being called 'European Union.' The Union's competence would embrace defence, foreign policy, and the protection of human rights. Although the decade that followed was one of relative stagnation so far as Community development was concerned, the Delors initiative from 1985 with the SEA, the dash for the single market and the inevitability of the further development of procedures and practices to implement Title III represent the addition of a huge new increment of Europeanization.

Might the time have come when the adjective sovereign in

Article 5 is no longer appropriate? Discussing this point as long ago as 1966 John Temple Lang wrote:

> Since sovereignty is not a precise concept, it is not possible to say exactly at what point in the process of political integration member states would cease to be sovereign, but as long as foreign policy and defence are not assigned, the member states remain sovereign and independent.[42]

Under the SEA, foreign policy is now virtually assigned. Foreign policy can involve security and security embraces defence. Already the device of using another international umbrella organization such as the Western European Union or NATO, is wearing thin and the other member states might not be willing to pander forever to Irish inhibitions. Faced with this situation the Irish government and Irish people generally might do worse than reflect on the words of a government White Paper in 1972:

> Such limitations on national freedom of action which membership of the Communities will involve for us will be more than counter-balanced by the influence which we will be able to bring to bear on the formulation of Community policies affecting our interests. We must contrast this with our present position as a very small country, independent but with little or no capacity to influence events abroad that significantly affect us.[43]

Eventually, legal sanction will have to be given to the end of what is already a political anachronism. In the circumstances of 1937, it no doubt seemed important to declare that Ireland was a sovereign state: to many today it does not.

9

Politicians and the Constitution

A T THE BEGINNING of this book, it was suggested that, ideally, a constitution should be 'normative', i.e. not only valid in a legal sense but in itself a political force, in the words of Karl Loewenstein, 'like a suit that fits and is actually worn.'[1] To achieve and maintain this desirable characteristic, it was argued, a constitution needs to be developed in such a way as to reflect the community's experiences and the changes in its culture. As time goes by, the suit might well need to be adjusted; a button moved on the jacket, the trousers let out a bit perhaps etc.

There is no doubt that the process of judicial review provides one means of doing this. It is a valuable 'mechanism of incremental adaptation'[2]. However, sometimes, more than that is needed. Indeed, the more active and creative the judiciary, the less the basic document itself expresses the actual position in constitutional law. This is particularly the case when judges become innovative or policy-oriented or, as has happened in Ireland, discover 'undisclosed' human rights. It might well be true, as many say, that *Bunreacht na hEireann* has served well. It does not follow as some, including particularly some lawyers, argue, that it does not need systematic amendment but ought to be left to lawyers to develop in case law *ad infinitum*.

The 'mechanism of judicial tuning', as Daniel Elazar called it,[3] has other limitations, not least on account of the judges' lack of accountability. As Cass Sunstein observed, this becomes a serious matter in a democracy where, as has occurred, constitutional courts have assumed what he called a 'deliberative' function through the process of constitutional adjudication:

Many of the problems raised by judicial review derive from the discretionary character of interpretation.... In these cases, the problem for constitutional democracy is why the discretionary power necessarily implied by this interpretive task should be conferred on unelected judges.[4]

This is a handicap that becomes the more obvious when the courts take decisions that clearly amount to policy making rather than filling in the interstices in policy, for policy making is a function that belongs properly to others.

From the very beginning de Valera was quite specific on this matter. When he was explaining and defending his draft proposals in the Dáil he argued that it was 'the Oireachtas that has the responsibility of working in the public interest and of seeing in the passing of its laws, that the rights of the individual ... and the rights of the community ... do not conflict and are properly coordinated.'[5] Populist leader as he then was, he had a considerable suspicion of the judges because of their origins and their traditions. Clearly, he intended that politicians and only politicians should have the right — and the duty — to formulate changes, with the people having the final say by referendum: 'it ought to be the people alone who would change it.'[6]

However, amending *Bunreacht na hEireann* was not an important issue for de Valera. On the contrary, in his view it was a great achievement to have at last given his country a settled framework within which political life could be carried on. It is true, as the distinguished political journalist, Michael McInerney subsequently recalled, that after endless hours of drafting, negotiations and advocacy, he could still concede that 'of course, the Constitution might not last' and one day perhaps would have to be changed. He could hardly have envisaged circumstances in which any important change was likely however. Indeed, he had gone to considerable pains to formulate key articles in such a way as to ensure that even the most momentous changes, viz. breaking the link with the British Crown and formally declaring the state to be a republic, could be effected without amendments being needed. He had, too, with great difficulty and skill found a compromise form of words on church-state relations which, if it did not please some local Catholic bishops, did not evoke the open hostility of the Church. In any case, it soon became clear that de Valera had on the whole 'got it right': it did suit the people (of the twenty-six counties at least). In an increasingly conservative epoch, he and they came to view *Bunreacht na hEireann* as finished business. While he was in charge there would be few changes.

After a short transitional period during which, it was intended, tidying up changes could be made on the authority of the Oireachtas alone, *Bunreacht na hEireann* was to be a 'rigid' constitution i.e. to amend it would require special procedures involving the passage of a bill through the houses of the Oireachtas and, subsequently, its submission in a referendum to the verdict of the electorate. Provision for popular initiative i.e. the right of a specified number of citizens to propose an amendment and have it voted on, a device that had been in the Irish Free State Constitution, was not included. It had been removed in 1928 by the Cumann na nGaedheal government after Fianna Fáil had organized a petition for the removal of the oath of loyalty and it looked likely that it would be used. In power, de Valera thought less well of it. The people were to have the final say and that was enough.

II

Apart from two amendments effected under the Transitory Provisions of the Constitution, which were far from tidying up changes, being occasioned by the exigencies of World War II, no changes were formally proposed before 1958 and none were actually enacted until 1972.[7] From the late nineteen sixties, however, there was continual talk of amending and by a few even of replacing *Bunreacht na hEireann*. As we have seen, it was mostly occasioned by developments in three areas: first, the fundamental changes that occurred in Western Europe from the fifties, not least in the Catholic Church, and which slowly affected Ireland; second, the civil war in Northern Ireland that exacerbated the 'Northern problem'; and, third, Ireland's membership of the European Communities with the consequent imposition of a new system of law upon the domestic system. Consideration of amendments was often, in fact usually, in the context of contentious issues — church-state relations, Northern Ireland, and how to adapt to fulfil the obligations of membership of the Communities with a Constitution that in origin did not envisage such a burgeoning supra-national polity. It is because of this that constitutional development was difficult and deficient and caused deep divisions among those politicians, mostly leaders, who confronted these issues. For the same reason there developed an irresponsible, 'leave-it-to-the-courts-or-let-it-alone-and-it-will-go-away' attitude among rank and file public representatives.

A survey of the eight amendments enacted since 1972 shows how meagre has been the politicians' response to their obligation to develop *Bunreacht na hEireann* and to maintain its congruency with social and political realities. Membership of the European Communities occasioned two amendments (the third amendment in 1972 which allowed Ireland to join and the tenth in 1987 which authorised the state to ratify the Single European Act, as it was obliged in law to do[8]). That amendment and another, the sixth amendment, on adoption, were made necessary by Court decisions which forced the government and the Oireachtas to act. Not all by any means of the other changes can be ascribed to politicians carrying out their developmental duties. Those that were — the lowering of the voting age to eighteen (the fourth amendment in 1972); a change that permitted the addition of graduates of more third-level colleges to elect members to the Seanad (the seventh amendment in 1979) which was not put into operation; and the extension to non-citizens of the right to vote at Dáil elections (the ninth amendment in 1984) were uncontentious acts of political modernization. They represented the kind of changes that ought to be systematically considered in a routine procedure and, if found opportune, enacted. The remaining two were examples of a very different class of issue. Both were of great importance and both, significantly, owed their origin to Catholic interests. The deletion of the special position' clause in Article 44 in 1972 (the fifth amendment) was triggered by Cardinal Conway[9], and the so-called 'right-to-life amendment' to Article 40 (the eighth amendment) by Catholic pressure groups in 1983-4.[10]

This is a thin record for a period of over half a century during which Ireland changed dramatically; or at least it is if one accepts the argument made in this book about the need systematically to develop the Constitution. Many lawyers do not and, it has to be said, meagre change is not unusual in democratic countries. For example, the Constitution of the United States, admittedly a leaner document altogether, has been amended only twenty-six times in two hundred years, though perhaps it should have been changed more often.

The Irish experience of meagre change is, however, ironic when one considers that at the end of the de Valera era of political and constitutional stasis, his successor, Seán Lemass, made the case for regular, periodic reviews of the Constitution and set in train a procedure for this purpose. In other circumstances he might have been the initiator of a valuable piece of constitutional procedure that could have been repeated as and when necessary. The history of his initiative, its outcome, and the reactions to it are instructive. So, too, was the fate of Garret FitzGerald when, rather more brashly, he rode out on his 'constitutional crusade' in the early eighties. These experiences have salutary lessons for anyone interested in constitutional reform.

III

In a speech in March 1966 Seán Lemass, then Taoiseach, suggested that:

> the time had come for a general review of Bunreacht na hEireann. It is possible that some of the views regarding the procedures and institutional arrangements for applying the democratic principles on which the Constitution is framed, which prevailed thirty years ago, could now be modified in the light of our own experience or that of other countries in the intervening years.[11]

He accepted that the principles of the Constitution continued to have a strong appeal, but he argued that 'the manner in which these principles were expressed and the procedures by which it was decided to apply them might not ... be as suitable to our present requirements as they were... .' In any case, the Supreme Court had in some instances interpreted the Constitution 'in a way its drafters had not expected or intended.' He thought there was 'a case for carrying out a general review of the provisions of the Constitution.'[12] In the Dáil, a week later, he made it clear that he was thinking of this as a routine operation: such a review ought to be undertaken 'every twenty-five years or so.'[13]

This initiative was characteristic of Lemass's efforts to

modernize Irish government and public administration: at about the same time he also set up a body, the Public Service Organization Review Group, to review the structure of the public sector and the administration of public services. Perhaps, however, he had other motives too. In an interview subsequently, he identified two of the areas in which he thought there should be changes. He told Michael McInerney that:

> the Constitution had acted as a 'strait jacket', preventing many ideas from being implemented because of the new property safeguards and the attitude to the North.... 'After all there will always be a Northern Ireland government', he said. [14]

In August 1966, the three political parties represented in the Dáil agreed to 'an informal committee' of Deputies and Senators 'to review the constitutional, legislative and institutional bases of government.' In its report published in December 1967, this committee acknowledged that, in general, *Bunreacht na hEireann* was still regarded as satisfactory: 'we are not aware of any public demand for a change in the basic structure of the Constitution.'[15] However, it systematically reviewed the whole text and dealt with twenty-seven matters either by way of recommendation where the members were unanimous or, where they were not, by deploying the arguments for and against changes, 'leaving it to the government of the day to decide the items which should be selected for inclusion in any legislative proposals that may emerge.'[16]

This, intended by the committee to be an 'interim' report, was their only report. The traditionalists in Fianna Fáil — and there were many of them — were far behind their more progressive and realistic party colleagues on the committee, men like George Colley, its chairman, who saw the need to make changes if there was to be any hope at all of doing business with Unionists. The report was silently disowned.[17] Any hopes of subsequent implementation were thus dashed: they were completely buried by the subsequent decision of the Fianna Fáil government to go forward on one of the highly contentious issues dealt with in the report, namely the election system on which the committee had been unable to agree. The government in turn was rebuffed by the electorate at the subsequent referendum. The all-party approach to constitutional change was thus shattered and in spite of another half-hearted attempt to initiate reform by way of a similar committee in 1972, it was never renewed. By this time, many politicians, particularly the conservatives in the rank and file of the parliamentary parties had come to the view that changes requiring legislation, constitutional and other, which would be politically hazardous were best left to the courts which had in fact become very active and innovative from the middle nineteen sixties.[18] Denis Coghlan, political correspondent of *The Irish Times,* put it thus:

> The role of the Supreme Court as the guardian of the Constitution ... massaged the political cowardice of politicians in the past and encouraged them to avoid their legislative responsibility.
> The comfortable conviction grew up that legislation on difficult and dangerous social issues could await the imprimatur of the Supreme Court and that direct Constitutional reform should be avoided.[19]

This attitude which endured into and through the eighties was not confined to 'social' issues as Coghlan called them. In 1986, Patrick MacEntee, the Chairman of the Bar Council, told a summer school on 'The Law and the People':

> I conclude that the legislature has been disposed to vacate certain areas of their legislative functions where unpopular decisions were for one reason or another unavoidable.[20]

He cited two recent cases, the McGlinchey and Shannon cases, in which the Supreme Court 'had been led into areas of policy-making and legislation', for it had by its decisions 'substantially amended the Extradition Act of 1965'. He commented that:

> not alone did the court substantially change the law without reference to the Oireachtas, but neither House complained — on the contrary everyone seemed pleased that the Supreme Court had grasped the nettle and obviated the need for debate or decisions in Oireachtas na hEireann.[21]

The episode of amending Article 44 in 1972 revealed a less appealing side of politicians' prudence when it came to be combined with opportunism. Rushing through the door opened for them by Cardinal Conway, Deputies fell over one another to suggest that they had been in favour of the change all along, especially as a contribution to removing misconceptions held in Northern Ireland and elsewhere about the nature of the Republic. Speakers from all parties claimed that the existing provisions were and always had been otiose. The change 'has our support mainly because we think it should never have been in the Constitution': it had been a Fianna Fáil mistake in 1937: it was 'a wholly unnecessary irritant which has given to the opponents of this state a stick with which to beat it': 'the change had been sought by the Labour Party for some time.'[22] In the excitement, some spokesmen of all parties urged the need for an entirely new Constitution. This was put most strongly by a Fine Gael speaker, Deputy Richie Ryan, who declared 'that we in Fine Gael urge that the present Constitution should be scrapped at the earliest possible date and replaced by a modern, more efficient and honest document.'[23] However, as we have seen, the Church closed that door again: Fianna Fáil had already closed the other one; and that was that for a decade.

IV

Attention has already been drawn to Garret FitzGerald's views in *Towards a New Ireland* (1972) on what needed to be done to tackle the Northern Ireland problem and at the same time to make the Republic a more pluralist society.[24] A decade later, as Taoiseach, he was in a position to take the necessary initiatives. He lost no time in doing so: perhaps he was hasty. In a radio interview on 27 September 1981, three months after his election to office and without consulting the Opposition, he declared his intention of mounting a 'constitutional crusade' aimed at eliminating the sectarian and confessional nature of some parts of *Bunreacht na hEireann* and replacing them with pluralist principles.[25] His avowed purpose was to seek to allay the suspicions of Northerners and in this connection he referred particularly to Articles 2, 3 and 41 (the Article on the Family which contains the provision preventing divorce legislation). The subsequent Seanad motion, introduced at the earliest opportunity, at the first meeting of the new session in October, referred to 'the desirability of creating within this island conditions favourable to unity through a reconciliation of its people.' To this end it was proposed to undertake 'a constitutional and legislative review.'[26]

By the time that motion was moved, the proposal had been rejected out of hand by the Fianna Fáil leader, Charles Haughey, who had already accused FitzGerald of selling the pass on national unity:

> I regard it as a serious undermining of our national position — the equivalent of sabotage of our national policy of unity — to attack the Constitution in the way that Dr FitzGerald has done, to attack the bona fides of politicians of all parties in the South and to attempt to suggest that our State has a sectarian basis. [27]

It was already too late for FitzGerald to quote (as he subsequently did) Cardinal Ó Fiaich, Conway's successor, who had some years before complained that 'Southern politicians should have been working for the past ten years on a Constitution which would be acceptable to both Protestants and Catholics.'[28] There would be no review: the Fianna Fáil side of the double doors remained tightly shut. When, later, FitzGerald attempted, first, to have a moderate 'right to life' amendment substituted for the Catholic pressure groups' stronger version and, second, to amend Article 41 to permit divorce in certain circumstances, the Church — Cardinal Ó Fiaich's remarks notwithstanding — with the support of Fianna Fáil, saw to it that the other door was kept closed too and he was defeated on both counts. [29]

He suffered the same fate in the wider arena of the New Ireland Forum of which mention has already been made. [30] The aim of that venture was to address the Northern Ireland problem in a positive and constructive fashion by compromise and consent. Its members were all politicians. In the case of the parties in the Republic, they were all leaders of the main parties in the Oireachtas: in the case of the Social Democratic and Labour Party, the only Northern party to take up the offer of membership, its leading members. In the course of its work, it involved a wide range of civil and religious leaders, experts and others and it commissioned papers on economic, legal and other aspects of the situation in Ireland, north and south.

In its way the New Ireland Forum was a systematic effort to review the constitutional situation, albeit in a much wider — and more hypothetical — context, that of 'a new Ireland' as its Report put it.

> It is clear that a new Ireland will require a new Constitution which will ensure that the needs of all traditions are fully

met. Society in Ireland as a whole comprises a wider diversity
of cultural and political traditions than exists in the South,
and the Constitution and laws of a new Ireland must
accommodate these social and political realities.[31]

Although the Report did not review *Bunreacht na hEireann* as such,
it proceeded from an historical and analytical survey of Irish
circumstances to identify the 'major realities' of the situation and
to list the 'necessary elements' of a framework within which a new
Ireland could emerge.'[32] It outlined a preferred political form for
the new state, a unitary system, together with other possible forms.
The new state would require a 'non-denominational' constitution
and there would have to be constitutional guarantees of civil and
religious liberties that 'would entail no alteration nor diminution
of the provisions in respect of civil and religious liberties which
apply at present to the citizens of Northern Ireland.'[33]

From the beginning the Northern Unionist parties boycotted
the New Ireland Forum and denounced its Report. On the other
side, the Fianna Fáil leader, Charles Haughey, in effect extinguished
what little life there might have been in it with his strong statement,
on the very day it was published, denying Unionists the right to
stand out against nationalist aspirations and a unitary state.[34] It
was, then, a futile exercise but it had some value as a learning
process, exposing very clearly, as it did, the hard rocks of reality
that had still to be circumnavigated if ever the Northern problem
was to be solved. It contributed little or nothing to constitutional
development in the Republic.

The Lemass and FitzGerald initiatives are the major attempts
so far at giving systematic consideration to changing the
Constitution. One other deserves mention not least, as in the case
of Lemass and FitzGerald, because of the outcome, or at least the
immediate outcome. In January 1988, the Progressive Democrats,
self-styled and genuinely aspirant 'mould breakers' of Irish politics
and proponents of radical change, published their proposals in the
form of a draft of a Constitution for a New Republic together
with an explanatory memorandum.[35] The party leader, Desmond
O'Malley, said that they had put it out for public discussion and
it was their intention to move a Private Member's Bill later in the
year[36]. It was a highly professional piece of work. At the time the
party had fourteen seats (8.5%) in Dáil Eireann and hoped to play
a key role in the future, as indeed they soon did. What followed

was significant. Firstly, it was ignored by politicians and public alike. Only the deliberate omission of mention of the Deity from the Preamble was immediately seized upon and became virtually the major talking point. Because the omission seemed likely to damn the whole venture and was unpopular with some of the party's members, the leadership had to backtrack.[37] Secondly, when after the general election in June 1989, the Progressive Democrats held the balance of power, part of the price they paid to enter a coalition government with Fianna Fáil was to forgo the inclusion of constitutional reform on the policy agenda for the duration.[38]

V

The lessons of these experiences are clear. Firstly, in the Irish situation, bipartisan agreement between the major parties is a prerequisite of successful constitutional change in areas of great public concern. Obviously these include Northern Ireland, church-state relations and any proposals which raise moral issues; and there might be others too. With Fianna Fáil enjoying the support of between forty and fifty per cent of the electorate at every election, no initiatives by other parties could hope to succeed without its approval. Fianna Fáil's own experience when it tried unsuccessfully to alter the election system in 1959 and 1968 suggests that the reverse is also true. In practice, this has meant that there is a veto not only on change but even on discussing the possibility of change for, from the early seventies, it was Fianna Fáil policy that the time to discuss change was when elected representatives of North and South were seated around a table to discuss the future of the country and not before. That policy has not altered in almost twenty years. Secondly, to propose changing the words of Article 2 or 3 was in the past to arouse deep emotions of hostility among many people, not only in Fianna Fáil, a feeling enhanced by the pietistic reverence among the Fianna Fáil faithful for the text devised by de Valera. Perhaps time and a greater understanding and awareness of Northern Ireland realities are changing this, but it will take more time yet in the Fianna Fáil heartland. Thirdly, to propose reforms such as the legalization of divorce aimed at making the Constitution an appropriate vehicle for a more pluralistic society carries the great political risk of provoking a *de facto* veto by the Catholic clergy whatever the Church's official view about the respective roles of church and state. Even in a Northern Ireland context where the bishops are prepared to see different rules for North and South, the process of getting agreed formulae would nevertheless be fraught with almost insurmountable difficulties.

It does not follow that there is no need for a systematic procedure to identify and elucidate points that might require attention and to process proposals for change as far as possible or expedient. In the case of *Bunreacht na hEireann* there are many matters that merit consideration apart from those great and contentious issues in the context of which most talk of change has so far taken place. Not all of them are trivial. Lemass was the only person to have initiated and got under way a procedure for systematic review. It sprang from what might be called a 'two-track' theory of democratic procedures. This involves making a clear distinction between methods suitable for constitution making and the kind of matters that go into constitutions, on the one hand, and lower track law making about routine issues, on the other, which are dealt with by the normal political processes. The rational-analytic processes of the Committee on the Constitution carried on in private with exchanges of papers, marshalling of facts, collection of comparative data, deployment of arguments pro and con, and culminating in tentative drafts, are more likely to produce a consensus if that is possible or a compromise if it is not, than a process that brings issues immediately into the public arena in a confrontational manner. Moreover, experience shows that this latter way of proceeding almost always slows down some kinds of changes even when, privately, many politicians think that they are desirable.

The Committee on the Constitution was composed of leading members of the parliamentary parties, a format that ought to have increased the likelihood that agreement among them would augur well for eventual success. That it did not in this instance might not have been due to a weakness of the method. It arose partly no doubt because Lemass had left office before the process got very far and his leaving precipitated faction fighting in the party. Perhaps also the members, particularly those who belonged to Fianna Fáil, misjudged opinion in the party.

Some argue, however, that an all-party committee of Oireachtas members, whether formal or informal, is not the way to go about changing the Constitution. John Rogers, SC, a former Attorney General, is one of them:

> Such a review should be carried out in the first instance on a rational and coherent basis by an inter-disciplinary group with the competence to report in the broadest manner possible on the nature, operation and effect of the Constitution and its institutions in the life of the nation.
>
> It is submitted that the effect of the numerous Constitutional amendments, in particular that endorsing our membership of the Community together with the numerous important constitutional decisions of the courts since the early 1960s, require such a group to comprise of senior politicians with experience and familiarity with the operation of our Constitution along with persons other than politicians with a complete understanding of our constitutional law and political institutions.
>
> Such a group should be established formally pursuant to an Act of the Oireachtas which would give to the group the status of an independent Constitutional convention. . . .
>
> The Chairman might be the President for the time being of the Law Reform Commission and that body might be utilised as a resource for the Convention.[39]

It might be argued that this approach is too rationalistic, too 'academic' and too far removed from the hard realities of party politics. Perhaps Keith Banting and Richard Simeon are right when they say, in their *Introduction to The Politics of Constitutional Change in Industrial Nations,* that 'constitution-making is not an exercise in value-free problem solving; nor is it usually a search for a set of words which enshrines a pre-existing consensus.'[40] Sometimes, as they rightly point out, 'the demand for constitutional change itself represents lack of consensus about some important aspects of the system. . . . Lack of consensus makes constitutional change necessary. The same lack makes resolution supremely difficult.'[41] No one can doubt that this is the case in respect of some issues in Ireland.

Some issues, but not all by any means. The need to update the text of *Bunreacht na hEireann* by incorporating changes that have in effect already been made by the courts and by coming to terms with the consequences of Community membership, cited by Rogers above, are among them. This kind of change is very appropriate material for the rational-analytic approach suggested by him. The same approach would at least maximize the possibility

of reaching a consensus or effecting compromises that all parties
could go out and sell. Where consensus and compromise are not
possible, the very process itself of establishing this should promote
a recognition of the fact that a particular proposal is not at the
time practical politics before the issue provokes a political
confrontation in the public arena, thus providing fodder for the
media who will heighten it and a stage for pressure groups with
their sectional objectives.

In 1987, a distinguished political journalist, Bruce Arnold,
ruminating on *Bunreacht na hEireann* fifty years on, found it:

> not quite as benign as once we thought it to be.
>
> It is a bit like a beast in a cage, this Constitution, a
> supposedly gentle giant, created half a century ago, to protect
> us in a vast range of different ways, and now found to have
> a will of its own not quite constructed as once we thought....
> Instead of being benign, and increasingly biddable, the beast
> in the cage is becoming something of a handful. It has shown
> a capacity for embarassing us in Europe. It is a weapon to
> which citizens increasingly feel they have recourse. It offers
> bizarre potential. It may well be invoked against the Anglo-
> Irish Agreement, bringing further difficulty.[42]

He could easily have added other examples and they continue to
arise. For example, in the summer of 1989, it seemed likely that
a new Community treaty would soon be framed providing for a
common currency and a European Central Bank. Ireland might
not be able to ratify it for the government and Oireachtas have
failed so far to consider the implications of the Crotty case which
has dropped off the political agenda for the moment. This would
put it back on top as a matter of urgency. We should echo Arnold's
plea: 'Let us keep the beast we know, caged, but *alive*.'[43] (Author's
italics).

Select
Bibliography

On constitutions in general

K. G. Banting and
R. Simeon (eds),
The Politics of Constitutional Change in Industrial Nations: Redesigning the State (London, 1985).

J. Elster and R.
Slagstad (eds),
Constitutionalism and Democracy (Cambridge, 1988).

Carl J. Friedrich,
'The Constitution as a Political Force' and 'The Political Theory of the New Democratic Constitutions', both in H. E. Eckstein and D. E. Apter (eds), *Comparative Politics* (Glencoe, 1963).

K. Loewenstein,
'Reflections on the Value of Constitutions in Our Revolutionary Age', in H. E. Eckstein and D. E. Apter (eds), *Comparative Politics* (Glencoe, 1963).

E. McWhinney,
Constitution-making: Principles and Practice (Toronto and London, 1981).

J. R. Pennock and
J. W. Chapman
(eds),
Constitutionalism (New York, 1979).

K. C. Wheare,
Modern Constitutions, 2nd ed. (London, 1966).

Bunreacht na hEireann and the Constitutional Law of Ireland

J. Casey,
Constitutional Law in Ireland (London, 1987).

B. Doolan,   *Constitutional Law and Constitutional Rights in Ireland,* 2nd ed. (Dublin, 1988).

M. Forde,   *Constitutional Law of Ireland* (Cork and Dublin, 1987).

J. M. Kelly,   *The Irish Constitution,* 2nd ed. (Dublin, 1984).

J. M. Kelly with G.   *The Irish Constitution: Supplement to the*
W. Hogan and G.   *Second Edition* (Dublin, 1987).
Whyte,

D. G. Morgan,   *Constitutional Law of Ireland,* 2nd ed. (Blackrock, 1990).

J. O'Reilly and M.   *Cases and Materials on the Irish Constitution*
Redmond,   (Dublin, 1980).

Irish constitutional history and development

L. P. Beth,   *The Development of Judicial Review in Ireland 1937-1966* (Dublin, 1967).

J. Bowman,   *de Valera and the Ulster Question 1917-1973* (Oxford, 1982).

D. M. Clarke,   'The Role of Natural Law in Irish Constitutional Law' in *Irish Jurist,* vol. 17, new series (1982).

J. Cooney,   *The Crozier and the Dáil: Church and State in Ireland 1922-1986* (Cork & Dublin, 1986).

B. Farrell (ed.),   *de Valera's Constitution and Ours* (Dublin, 1988).

G. FitzGerald,   *Towards a new Ireland* (Dublin, 1973).

G. W. Hogan,   'Irish Nationalism as a Legal Ideology' in *Studies,* vol. 75 (1986).

G. W. Hogan,   'Law and Religion: Church-state Relations in Ireland from Independence to the Present Day' in *American Journal of Comparative Law,* vol. 35 (1987).

G. W. Hogan, 'The Supreme Court and the Single European Act', in *The Irish Jurist*, Vol 22, new series, Part I (1987), pp. 55-70.

G. W. Hogan, 'Legal Aspects of Church-State Relations in Ireland' in *St Louis University Public Law Review,* vol. 7 (1988).

F. Litton (ed.), *The Constitution of Ireland 1937-1987* (Dublin, 1988).

F. Murphy, 'The Single European Act' in *Irish Jurist,* Vol. 20, new series (1985).
New Ireland Forum Report (Dublin, 1984).

C. C. O'Brien, *States of Ireland* (London, 1972).

T. P. O'Mahony, *The Politics of Dishonour: Ireland 1916-1977* (Dublin, 1977).
Report of the Committee on the Constitution (Dublin, 1967).

J. Temple Lang, 'European Community Constitutional Law: the division of power between The Community and Member States' in *Northern Ireland Legal Quarterly,* vol. 39, pp. 209-34 (1988).

J. Temple Lang, 'European Community Law, Irish Law and the Irish Legal Profession' in *Dublin University Law Journal,* New Series, vol. 5, (1983).

J. H. Whyte, *Church and State in Modern Ireland 1923-1979,* 2nd ed. (Dublin, 1980).

J. H. Whyte, 'Recent Developments in Church-state Relations' in *Seirbhís Phoiblí,* vol. 6, no. 3 (Dublin, Autumn, 1985).

Notes to
Chapters

1

1. K. C. Wheare, *Modern Constitutions* (London, 1966), p. 2
2. S. A. de Smith, *Constitutional and Administrative Law,* 3rd ed., (Harmondsworth, 1977), p. 16.
3. *Ibid.,* p. 15.
4. O. Hood Phillips, *Constitutional and Administrative Law,* 6th ed., (London, 1978), p. 5.
5. P. Norton, *The Constitution in Flux* (Oxford, 1982), pp. 3–4.
6. C. J. Friedrich, *Limited Government* (Englewood Cliffs, 1947), p. 11.
7. S. A. de Smith, *op.cit.*, p. 18.
8. C. J. Friedrich, *Man and his Government* (New York, 1963), p. 217.
9. C. J. Friedrich, *Limited Government* (Englewood Cliffs, 1974), p. 4.
10. *The Federalist Papers* (Mentor Books, 1961), p. 322.
11. G. J. Schuchet in J. R. Pennock and J. W. Chapman (eds.) *Constitutionalism* (New York, 1979), p. 4.
12. See K. Loewenstein, *Political Power and the Governmental Process,* 2nd ed., (Chicago and London, 1965)., pp. 147–53.
13. *Ibid.,* p. 137.
14. E. McWhinney, *Constitution-making: Principles, Process, Practice* (Toronto, 1981), p. 7.

2

1. B. Farrell, *The Founding of Dáil Eireann: Parliament and Nation Building* (Dublin, 1971), p. xv.
2. F. Munger, *The Legitimacy of Opposition: The Change of Government in Ireland in 1932* (London, 1975), p. 6
3. Farrell, *op.cit.*, p. xv.
4. F. A. Ogg, *English Government and Politics*, 2nd ed. (New York, 1936), p. 731.

5. *Collected Works of Padraic H. Pearse: Political Writings and Speeches* (Dublin, 1924), pp. 231-2.
6. *Dáil Eireann, (Official Report:) Debates on the Treaty between Great Britain and Ireland* (Dublin 1922), p. 32 (19 December 1921).
7. *House of Commons Debates,* vol. 458, cols.1414-15 (25 November 1948).
8. M. Laffan, *The Partition of Ireland 1911-25* (Dundalk, 1983), p. 82.
9. *Ibid.,* p. 88.
10. *Ibid.,* p.116.
11. *Report of the Commission of Enquiry into the Civil Service,1932-35* (Dublin, 1935), para. 8.
12. J. Blanchard, *Le droit ecclésiastique contemporain d'Irlande* (Paris, 1958), p.11.

3

1. John Bowman, *De Valera and the Ulster Question 1917–1973* (Oxford, 1982), p. 147.
2. See B. Kennedy, 'The Special Position of John Hearne' in *Irish Times,* 8 April 1987.
3. See D. Keogh, 'The Constitutional Revolution: An Analysis of the Making of the Constitution' in F. Litton (ed.), *The Constitution of Ireland 1937–1987* (Dublin, 1988), pp. 4–84.
4. Bowman, op.cit., p. 3.
5. *Shorter Oxford English Dictionary,* 2nd ed. Quoted by de Valera in *Dáil Debates,* vol. 97, col. 2571 (17 July 1945).
6. That was the intention at least. In fact only five out of the ten presidential elections have involved a contest. On the other occasions the political parties have conspired to produce an agreed candidate.
7. *Dáil Debates,* vol. 68, col. 430 (14 June 1937).
8. Extracts from Document No. 2 (January 1922) as reproduced in D. Macardle, *The Irish Republic* (4th edition, Dublin, 1951), pp. 959-60.
9. Constitution (Amendment No. 27) Act and the Executive Authority (External Relations), Act 1936 (No. 58).
10. See *Dáil Debates,* Vol. 97, cols. 2568-74 (17 July 1945).
11. C. O'Leary, *The Irish Republic and its Experiment with Proportional Representation* (Notre Dame, 1961), p. 30.
12. *Dáil Debates,* vol.67, col. 60 (11 May 1937)
13. John Bowman, *op.cit.,* p. 268.
14. Bowman, *op.cit.,* p. 268 and p. 273. The quotation from Frank Gallagher is in the Gallagher, papers. MS 18, 375 (6). This is an unpublished draft of an attempted biography written with de Valera's cooperation which Bowman consulted.

15. Bowman, *op.cit.,* p. 281.
16. *Ibid.,* pp. 282-3.
17. Speech in November 1957 quoted in Bowman, p. 186.
18. Bowman, op. cit., p. 316.
19. John Whyte, *Church and State in Modern Ireland 1923-1979,* (2nd edition, Dublin, 1980), p. 36.
20. *Ibid.*
21. *Ibid.,* p. 40.
22. Extract from a St Patrick's Day broadcast quoted in Whyte, *op.cit.,* p. 48.
23. *Ibid.,* p. 50.
24. Garret FitzGerald in an interview with Geraldine Kennedy in *The Irish Times,* 29 December 1977.
25. The Earl of Longford and T. P. O'Neill, *Eamon de Valera,* (Dublin and London, 1970), p. 297.
26. See T. O'Neill and P. O'Fiannachta, *De Valera,* vol. 2 (Dublin, 1970), p. 337; Longford and O'Neill, *op. cit.,* p. 296.
27. Longford and O'Neill, *ibid.*
28. Pope Leo XIII, *Immortale Dei* (1885), English translation in *The Pope and the People, Select Letters and Addresses on Social Questions,* (London, 1943), p. 48.
29. Article 42.3 of 'Preliminary Draft' as circulated privately by de Valera, s. 9715A. Some Irish clergy opposed the de Valera approach as not being sufficiently Catholic 'but they were not in a position to do or say anything. The Vatican had given its tacit approval to the document.' D. Keogh in F. Litton (ed.), *The Constitution of Ireland 1937-1987* (Dublin, 1988), p. 59.
30. C.C. O'Brien, *States of Ireland,* (St Albans, 1974), p. 116.
31. Longford and O'Neill, *op. cit.,* p. 459.
32. See Bowman, *op. cit.,* p.311.
33. Longford and O'Neill, *op.cit.,* p. 459.
34. *Ibid.*
35. H. Shearman, *Anglo-Irish Relations* (London, 1948), p. 241.
36. Longford and O'Neill, *op.cit.,* pp. 459-60.
37. See below, p. 81, for Senator Eoin Ryan's opinion on de Valera's understanding of Northerners.
38. Bowman, *op.cit.,* pp. 127-8.

4

1. Quoted in *Irish Press,* 24 June 1937.
2. D. Martin, *A General Theory of Secularization,* (Oxford, 1978), p. 107.
3. *Ibid.,* p. 55.
4. *Ibid.,* p. 107.

5. In M. Fogarty, L. Ryan and J. Lee, *Irish Values and Attitudes: The Irish Report of the European Value Systems Study* (Dublin, 1984), p. 102.

6. J. Hickey, 'The Role of the Churches in the Conflict in Northern Ireland', in *Studies,* 74 (1985), p. 405.

7. Quoted in *The Irish Times.* 13 April 1955.

8. John Whyte, *Church and State in Modern Ireland, 1923-1979,* 2nd ed., (Dublin, 1980), p. 230.

9. *Dáil Debates,* vol. 125, cols. 739 and 784 (12 April, 1951).

10. Whyte, *op.cit.,* p. 231.

11. *Ibid.,* p. 160.

12. *Ibid.,* p. 171.

13. *Irish Catholic Directory,* 1951, p. 745.

14. C. Cruise O'Brien, *States of Ireland,* (London, 1972), p. 127.

15. J. Whyte, 'Recent Developments in Church-state Relations', in *Seirbhís Phoiblí,* vol. 6, no. 3, p. 4. (Autumn 1985),

16. J. Whyte, *Church and State in Modern Ireland, 1923-1979,* 2nd ed., (Dublin, 1980), p. 49.

17. D. Costello, 'The Natural Law and the Constitution' in *Studies,* vol. 45, (1956), p. 414.

18. Patrick McGilligan, a Senior Counsel, and former minister and Attorney General; and Vincent Grogan, then Parliamentary Draftsman. Both are quoted in J. Kelly, *Fundamental Rights in the Irish Law and Constitution,* 2nd ed., (Dublin, 1967), p. 65.

19. Quoted in G. M. Golding, *George Gavan Duffy 1882-1951: a Legal Biography,* (Blackrock, Co. Dublin, 1982), pp. 64 and 65.

20. Whyte, *op.cit.,* p. 167.

21. *The State (Ryan and Others)* v. *Lennon and Others* [1935], I.R. 70 at p. 205.

22. G. Hogan, 'Law and Religion: Church-state Relations in Ireland from Independence to the Present Day' in *American Journal of Comparative Law,* vol. 35, p. 56 (1987).

23. *In re Maguire; Maguire* v. *Attorney General* [1943] I.R. 238 at p. 254.

24. *Cook* v. *Carroll* [1945] I.R. 515 at p. 519.

25. *In re Tilson, Infants* [1951] I.R. 1 at p. 19.

26. *The Irish Times,* 12 December 1945.

27. E. McWhinney, *Judicial Review in the English-speaking World,* 4th ed., (Toronto, 1969), p. 173.

28. See below, pp. 52-9.

5

1. See D. Martin, *A General Theory of Secularization* (Oxford, 1978), pp. 2-3.
2. L. Ryan in M. Fogarty, L. Ryan and J. Lee, *Irish Values and Attitudes: The Irish Report of the European Value System Study*, (Dublin, 1984), p. 104.
3. Martin, *op.cit.,* pp. 270-79.
4. See M. Fogarty, et al., *Irish Values and Attitudes: The Irish Report of the European Value Systems Study,* (Dublin, 1984), ch. 2.
5. T. Inglis, 'Sacred and Secular in Catholic Ireland' in *Studies,* vol. 74 (1985), p. 40.
6. L. Ryan, *op.cit.,* pp. 101-102.
7. *Report of the Committee on the Constitution* (Stationery Office, Dublin, 1967), para. 136.
8. *Ibid.*
9. Reported in *The Irish Times,* 23 September 1969.
10. Deputy Richie Ryan, *Dáil Debates,* Vol. 263, col. 453 (2 November 1972)
11. *Statement of the Irish Episcopal Conference*, 25 November 1973.
12. *New Ireland Forum, Report of Proceedings,* 9 February 1984, p. 2.
13. J. Whyte, *Church and State in Modern Ireland 1923–1979,* 2nd ed., (Dublin, 1980), p. 368.
14. *New Ireland Forum, Report of Proceedings,* 9 February 1984, p. 2.
15. Bishop Jeremiah Newman, quoted in J. Cooney, *The Crozier and the Dáil: Church and State 1922–1986,* (Cork and Dublin, 1986), p. 106.
16. Newman, quoted in *The Irish Times,* 1 June 1976.
17. *Dáil Debates,* Vol. 312, col. 335, 28 February 1979.
18. J. Whyte, 'Recent Developments in Church-state Relations' in *Seirbhís Phoiblí,* vol. 6, no. 3 (1985), p. 4.
19. Quoted in *The Irish Times,* 17 March 1983.
20. Quoted in J. Cooney, *The Crozier and the Dáil: Church and State 1922–1986* (Cork, 1986), p. 61.
21. *Ibid,* p. 68.
22. Quoted *ibid.,* p. 104.
23. Michael O'Leary in *Irish Independent*, 4 October 1985.
24. Cardinal Thomas Ó Fiaich quoted in Cooney, *op. cit.,* p. 123.
25. *Ibid.*
26. Quoted in *The Irish Times,* 23 June 1986.
27. 'Divorce Poll: a Re-run of 1983 Referendum', *The Irish Times*, 3 July 1986.
28. *Ibid.,*
29. *MRBI 21st Anniversary Poll* (Market Research Bureau of

Ireland, Dublin, 1983), p. 15. See also the MRBI's 25th
Anniversary Survey, *Eire Inniu* (Dublin, 1987), pp. 13–14.

6

1. L. P. Beth, *The Development of Judicial Review in Ireland,
   1937-1966,* (Dublin, 1967), p. 1.
2. [1977] I.R. 159 at p. 176.
3. *Dáil Debates,* vol. 67, col. 69 (11 May 1937).
4. [1983] I.R.82 at p. 87.
5. K. C. Wheare, *Modern Constitutions,* (London, 1966), p. 105.
6. See J. M. Kelly, *The Irish Constitution* 2nd ed. (Dublin, 1980)
   and J. M. Kelly, with G. W. Hogan and G. Whyte, *The Irish
   Constitution, Supplement to the Second Edition* (Dublin, 1987).
   See also, J. O'Reilly and M. Redmond, *Cases and Materials
   on the Irish Constitution* (Dublin, 1980). Major textbooks of
   Irish constitutional law include J. Casey, *Constitutional Law
   in Ireland,* (London, 1987) and M. Forde, *Constitutional Law
   of Ireland,* (Cork and Dublin, 1987).
7. E. McWhinney, *Judicial Review in the English-speaking World,*
   4th ed. (Toronto, 1969), pp. 158 and 172.
8. L. P. Beth, *The Development of Judicial Review in Ireland,
   1937-1966* (Dublin, 1967), p. 3.
9. *In re Article 26 of the Constitution and the Offences against
   the State (Amendment) Bill,* 1940 [1940] I.R. 470 at p. 481.
10. *Pigs Marketing Board* v. *Donnelly (Dublin) Ltd.* [1939] I.R.
    413 at p. 418.
11. G. Horgan, 'Irish Nationalism as a Legal Ideology', in *Studies,*
    vol. 75, pp. 528 and 531 (Winter, 1986).
12. On p. 25.
13. Hogan, loc. cit., p. 532.
14. J. P. Casey, 'Law and the Legal System 1957-82' in F. Litton
    (ed.), *Unequal Achievement, the Irish Experience 1957-1982*
    (Dublin, 1982), p. 267.
15. See L. P. Beth, *The Development of Judicial Review in Ireland,
    1937-1966* (Dublin, 1967), pp. 67-9.
16. Quoted by J. Carroll, 'Challenges to Constitution "increasing"',
    The Irish Times, 30 December 1987.
17. J. P. Casey, 'The Development of Constitutional Law under
    Chief Justice O Dálaigh', *Dublin University Law Journal,* 1978,
    p. 5.
18. *In re Article 26 of the Constitution and the Criminal Law
    (Jurisdiction) Bill 1975,* [1977] I.R. 129 at p. 147.
19. [1965] I.R. 294 at p. 312.
20. *The State (Burke)* v. *Lennon* [1940] I.R. 136 at p. 179.
21. [1984] I.R. 36 at p.96.

22. [1974] I.R. 284 at p.310.
23. R. F. V. Heuston, 'Personal Rights under the Irish Constitution', *Irish Jurist,* Vol. XI, new series, p. 221 (1976).
24. *The State (Gleeson)* v. *Minister for Defence* [1976] I.R. 280 at p. 295.
25. J. M. Kelly with G. W. Hogan and G. Whyte, *The Irish Constitution, Supplement to the Second Edition,* (Dublin, 1987), p. 5.
26. J. Casey, *Constitutional Law in Ireland* (London, 1987), p. 336.
27. See e.g. *East Donegal Co-op Ltd* v. *Attorney General* [1970] I.R. 317.
28 [1987] I.L.R.M. 400. For further discussion of this case, see below pp. 110-111.
29. G. Hogan, 'Irish Nationalism as a Legal Ideology' in *Studies,* vol. 75, p. 528 (Winter 1986).
30. *Ibid.*
31. B. M. E. McMahon, 'A Sense of Identity in the Irish Legal System' in J. Lee (ed.), *Ireland: Towards a Sense of Place,* (Cork, 1985), p. 39.
32. Hogan, *loc. cit.,* p. 528.
33. *Ibid.,* p. 536.
34. *Ibid.*
35. Quoted in *Ireland, The Weekly Bulletin of the Department of External Affairs,* no. 421, 13 October 1958.
36. See J. M. Kelly, *The Irish Constitution,* (Dublin, 1980), pp. 334 ff.
37. D. M. Clarke 'The Role of Natural Law in Irish Constitutional Law', *The Irish Jurist,* vol. XVII, new series, Part 2, pp. 214 and 219 (1982).
38. *Ibid.,* p. 189.
39. In J. O'Reilly and M. Redmond, *Cases and Materials on the Irish Constitution,* (Dublin, 1980), p. XII.
40. *Fundamental Rights in the Irish Law and Constitution,* 2nd ed., (Dublin, 1967), p. 42.
41. D. Gwynn Morgan, *The Irish Times,* 7.2.1980.
42. McMahon, *loc. cit.,* p. 38.
43. 'Personal Rights under the Irish Constitution', *The Irish Jurist,* Vol. XI, new series, p. 211 (1976).
44. [1987] 2 C.M.L.R. 657. For further discussion of this case see pp. 110-111 below.
45. A. Cox, *The Role of the Supreme Court in American Government,* (Oxford, 1976), p. 100.
46. *Ibid.,* p. 103.
47. See above, p.54.
48. For example, on the cases of *Russell* v. *Fanning* ([1981] I.R. 505) and *Finucane* v. *McMahon,* in 1990 (which overturned the *Russell* view).

49. G. Hogan, 'Law and Religion: Church-state Relations in Ireland from Independence to the Present Day' in *American Journal of Comparative Law,* vol. XXXV, p. 69 (1987).
50. See *ibid.,* p. 72, The euphemism was Michael O Morain's. He was Minister for Justice in 1970.
51. *Ibid.,* p. 74.
52. *Ibid.,* p. 88.
53. Quoted in J. O Reilly and M. Redmond, *Cases and Materials on the Irish Constitution,* (Dublin, 1980), p. xi.
54. G. Hogan in W. Duncan (ed.), *Law and Social Policy,* (Dublin, 1987), p. 75.
55. In J. O'Reilly and M. Redmond, *op.cit.,* p. xi.

7

1. Quoted in M. Laffan, *The Partition of Ireland 1911-25,* (Dundalk, 1983), p. 82.
2. J. M. Kelly, 'Law and Manifesto' in F. Litton (ed.), *The Constitution of Ireland 1937-1987,* (Dublin, 1988), p. 209.
3. See J. Bowman, *de Valera and the Ulster Question, 1917-1973,* (Oxford, 1982), pp. 29-30 and pp. 300 ff.
4. M. McInerney, 'Carrying on Fianna Fáil's Liberal Tradition: a Profile of Eoin Ryan', *The Irish Times,* 12 January 1972.
5. *Dáil Debates,* Vol. 67, col. 80 (11 May 1937).
6. Bowman, *op.cit.,* pp. 329 and 330.
7. J. Lynch quoted in Bowman, *op.cit.,* p. 326.
8. *Report of the Committee on the Constitution,* (December, 1967), para. 12.
9. *Ibid.,* para. 123.
10. *Ibid.,* para. 124
11. *Ibid.,* para. 136.
12. *Ibid.,* para. 139.
13. Reported in *The Irish Times,* 23 September 1969.
14. G. FitzGerald, *Towards a New Ireland,* (Dublin and London, 1973), p. viii.
15. *Ibid.,* p. 124.
16. *Ibid.,* p. 150 and p. 152.
17. *Ibid.,* p. 150.
18. *Ibid.*
19. *Ibid.*
20. *Seanad Debates,* vol. 96, cols. 179, 189 and 193. (9 October 1981)
21. *New Ireland Forum Report,* (Stationery Office, Dublin, 1984), para. 4.2 (p. 17).
22. *Ibid.,* para 4.6 (p. 19).
23. *Ibid.,* para. 4.13 (p. 23).

24. *Ibid.*, para. 4.6 (p. 19).
25. *Ibid.*, para 5.7 (p. 29)
26. *Irish Times,* 3 May 1984.
27. *Sunday Tribune,* 12 February 1984.
28. New Ireland Forum, Public Sessions, Thursday, 9 February, 1984, *Report of Proceedings,* (Stationery Office, Dublin, 1984), p. 2.
29. Submission made to the New Ireland Forum on behalf of the Irish Episcopal Conference reported in *The Irish Times,* 14 January 1984.
30. Market Research Bureau of Ireland Ltd, *Eire Inniu, an MRBI Perspective on Irish Society Today,* (Dublin, 1987), p. 48.
31. *Seanad Debates,* vol. 96, col. 185 (9 October 1981).
32. C. Carter, 'Permutations of Government' in *Administration,* Vol. 20, pp. 50-57 (1972). His article was a contribution to a symposium entitled 'The Irish Dimension' sponsored by the Irish Association.
33. H. Lauterpacht (ed.), *International Law, a Treatise* by L. Oppenheim, vol. 1, *Peace,* (London, 1967), pp. 452-3.
34. In *The Future of Northern Ireland. A Paper for Discussion* (HMSO, London, 1972).
35. *New Ireland Forum Report,* (Stationery Office, Dublin, 1984), paras. 8.1 — 8.5 (p. 37).
36. Final Draft Report of a New Ireland Forum Sub-Committee on Joint Authority. The report was not officially published but appeared in *The Irish Times,* 9 May 1984.
37. *New Ireland Forum Report,* para. 8.7 (p. 38).

8

1. J. Temple Lang, *The Common Market and Common Law* (Chicago and London, 1966), p. XI.
2. *H. P. Bulmer Ltd.* v. *J. Bollinger,* S.A. [1974] 1 ch. 401 at p. 418.
3. Carl J. Friedrich, 'The Political Theory of the New Democratic Constitutions', in H. E. Eckstein and D.E. Apter (eds) *Comparative Politics* (Glencoe, 1963), p. 145.
4. J. Temple Lang, 'Application of the Law of the European Communities in the Republic of Ireland', in *Die Erweiterung der Europaischen Gemeinschaften, Kolner Schriften zum Europarecht,* Band 15 (Carl Heymanns Verlag KG, 1972), p. 47.
5. *Ibid.*, p. 48
6. *Van Gend en Loos* v. *Netherlands Fiscal Administration* (Case 26/62) [1963] E.C. R. 1 at 12.

7. *Membership of the European Communities: Implications for Ireland* (Stationery Office, Dublin, 1970), pp. 2-4.
8. Quoted by John Temple Lang in 'European Community Constitutional Law: The Division of Power between the Community and Member States', in *Northern Ireland Legal Quarterly,* vol. 39, p. 231 (1988).
9. John Temple Lang, 'European Community Law, Irish Law and the Irish Legal Profession', *Dublin University Law Journal,* New Series, Vol. 5, (1983), p. 4.
10. Written Question No. 2109/87 in *Official Journal of the European Communities,* No. C 181/13 (11.7.88).
11. M. Forde, *Constitutional Law of Ireland* (Cork and Dublin, 1987), p. 222.
12. *Crotty* v. *An Taoiseach,* [1987] I.L.R.M. 400 at p. 446.
13. *Pubblico Ministero [of Italy]* v. *Ratti* (Case 148/78), [1979] E.C.R. 1629 at pp. 1641 ff.
14. For an example of a reference by an Irish court, see *Minister for Fisheries* v. *C. A. Schonenberg [and others]* (Case 88/77) [1978] E.C.R. 473. For an example of an Irish court accepting and applying a European Court ruling, see *Pigs and Bacon Commission* v. *Mc Carren and Co. Ltd.* [1981] I.R. 451.
15. See J. Temple Lang, 'European Community Law, Irish Law and the Irish Legal Profession', *Dublin University Law Journal,* New Series, Vol. 5, (1983), p. 3.
16. See the case of *Nold, J. K.G.* v. *E.C. Commission* (case 4/73) [1974] E.C.R. 491.
17. John Temple Lang, 'European Community Law, Irish Law and the Irish Legal Profession', *Dublin University Law Journal,* New Series, vol. 5 (1983), p. 3. See also *Northern Ireland Legal Quarterly,* vol. 40 (1989), p. 233.
18. John Temple Lang, 'European Community Constitutional Law: the Division of Powers between the Community and Member States', *Northern Ireland Legal Quarterly,* vol. 39, p. 209 (1988).
19. *Ibid.,* p. 217.
20. *Ibid.*
21. *Ibid.,* p. 214.
22. J. Temple Lang, 'Article 5 of the EEC Treaty: the Emergence of Constitutional Principles in the Case Law of the Court of Justice' in *Fordham International Law Journal,* vol. 10, p. 503 (1987).
23. E. Noël, 'The Single European Act' in *Government and Opposition,* vol. 24, p. 4 (Winter 1989).
24. *Ibid.,* p. 3.
25. Michael Forde, *Constitutional Law of Ireland,* (Cork and Dublin, 1987), p. 214.
26. *Crotty* v. *An Taoiseach* [1987] ILRM 400 at p. 444. See G. W. Hogan, 'The Supreme Court and The Single European Act'

in *The Irish Jurist,* Vol. XXII, new series, Part I (1987), pp. 55-70.

27. *Ibid.,* at p. 448.
28. Forde *op.cit.,* p. 217.
29. See particularly Dáil Debates, Vol. 371, cols. 2216 ff; (22 April 1987).
30. *Ibid.,* col. 2195
31. *The Irish Times,* 7 May 1987. See also Dáil Debates, Vol. 371, cols. 22 83 ff; (22 April 1987).
32. See *The Irish Times,* 17 November 1986 (Temple Lang) and 25 November 1986 (Robinson).
33. F. Murphy in *The Irish Times,* 'Court Decision goes beyond SEA' article in *The Irish Times,* 15 April 1987.
34. M. Forde, *Constitutional Law of Ireland,* (Cork and Dublin, 1987), p. 216.
35. F. Murphy, *The Irish Times,* 15 April 1987. Another distinguished constitutional lawyer, James Casey was among those who also took the view that the case raised 'grave doubts about the constitutional validity of the Anglo-Irish Agreement' (*Constitutional Law in Ireland,* (Dublin, 1987, p. 184). Notice, however, that this extrapolation to the Anglo-Irish Agreement seems to have been rejected by the High Court (*McGimpsey v. Ireland* [1988] I.R. 567 (H.C.) and, subsequently, the Supreme Court (1 March 1990).
36. *Ibid.*
37. Dáil Debates, Vol. 371, , col. 2221, (22 April 1987).
38. *Ibid.,* col. 2287. Dr FitzGerald was quoting from Mr de Valera's Dáil speech on 11 May 1937 (Dáil Debates, vol. 67, col. 60). So, too, had the Taoiseach, Charles Haughey, earlier in the same debate (*Ibid.,* cols. 2195-6).
39. *Ibid.,* col. 2289.
40. *Membership of the European Communities: Implications for Ireland* (Stationery Office, Dublin 1970), p. 5.
41. Case 48/71, *Commission* v. *Italy* [1972] ECR 532.
42. J. Temple Lang, *The Common Market and the Common Law* (Chicago and London, 1966), p. xi.
43. *The Accession of Ireland to the European Communities* (Stationery Office, Dublin, 1972), p. 59.

9

1. *Political Power and the Governmental Process,* 2nd ed., (Chicago and London, 1965), p. 137.
2. K. G. Banting and R. Simeon (eds), *The Politics of Constitutional Change in Industrial Nations: Redesigning the State* (London, 1985), p. 9.

3. In Banting and Simeon (eds), p. 233.
4. In J. Elster and R. Slagstad (eds), *Constitutionalism and Democracy* (Cambridge, 1988), p. 336.
5. *Dáil Debates,* vol. 67, col. 786 (3 June 1937).
6. *Dáil Debates,* vol. 68, col. 288 (10 June 1937)
7. The First Amendment Act defined and extended the meaning of the words 'time of war' in Article 28.3.3⁰ to include an emergency occasioned by a war in which the state was not a participant. During such an emergency the Government has certain additional powers. The Second Amendment Act included, in addition to a miscellaneous collection of tidying-up changes, a provision which permitted an emergency occasioned by a time of war or armed rebellion to be extended beyond the cessation of actual hostilities. Incredible as it might seem, Ireland was in 1991 still in such a state of emergency. The original Oireachtas resolution declaring it remained in force from 1939 to 1976 only to be succeeded, when doubts were raised about its legality, by another which still remained in force in 1991.
8. See pp. 99-100 above.
9. See pp. 49-50 above.
10. See pp. 54-55 above.
11. Speech delivered on 25 March 1966 and quoted in J. M. Kelly, 'Revision of the Constitution' in *The Irish Times,* 25-27 December 1967.
12. *Ibid.,* quoted in J. M. Kelly 'Revision of the Constitution of Ireland' in *The Irish Jurist,* vol. 1, New Series, p. 2 (1966).
13. *Dáil Debates,* vol. 222, col. 496 (31 March 1966).
14. Michael McInerney in a symposium entitled 'The Constititution 40 Years on' in *The Irish Times,* 30 December 1977.
15. *Report of the Committee on the Constitution,* December 1967, Pr 9817, Stationery Office, (Dublin, 1967), para. 8.
16. *Ibid.,* para. 5.
17. This committee's recommendations on Articles 2 and 3 and on other articles which were of concern in a Northern Ireland context are discussed on pp. 83-85 above.
18. See above, p. 73.
19. Quotations from his contribution to a symposium on the fiftieth anniversary of *Bunreacht na hEireann, The Irish Times,* 29 December 1987.
20. *The Irish Times,* 18 August 1986.
21. *Ibid.* The cases to which he referred were *McGlinchey* v. *Wren* [1982] I.R. 154 and *Shannon* v. *Fanning* [1985] I.L.R.M. 385. More recently, the Governemnt has shown how reluctant it is to have a review of extradition legislation carried out by the Oireachtas. See the statement to the Dáil by the Minister for Justice, *The Irish Times,* 26 April 1990.

22. See *Dáil Debates,* vol. 263, cols. 422-92, (2 November 1972).
23. See above, p. 50.
24. See above, pp. 86-87.
25. For FitzGerald's interview, see *The Irish Times,* 28 September 1981. Haughey's complaint about lack of consultation was made in a radio interview. See *The Irish Times,* 29 September 1981.
26. *Seanad Debates,* vol. 96, col. 17 (8 October 1981).
27. Statement made at a press conference on 28 September 1981 reported in *The Irish Times,* 29 September 1981.
28. Interview with *Belfast Telegraph* in 1977 quoted by FitzGerald. See *Seanad Debates,* vol. 96, col. 195 (9 October 1981).
29. See above, pp. 53-59.
30. See above, pp. 88-90.
31. *New Ireland Forum Report,* Stationery Office (Dublin, 1984), para. 4.14
32. *Ibid.,* para. 5.2
33. *Ibid.,* para, 6.1
34. Quoted above, p. 89
35. There are in fact three documents:- *Constitution for a New Republic; Explanatory Memorandum – Constitution for a New Republic; Notes on Decisions in the Drafting of the Constitution for a New Republic.* (In each case , Dublin, January 1988).
36. *The Irish Times,* 14 January 1988.
37. See *The Irish Times,* 13 September 1988.
38. See S. Kenny, *Go Dance on Somebody Else's Grave* (Dublin, 1990) p. 160.
39. John Rogers, 'Why it should not be Left to Politicians Alone', *Irish Press,* 15 July 1987.
40. K. G. Banting and R. Simeon (eds), *The Politics of Constitutional Change in Industrial Nations: Redesigning the State* (London, 1985), p. 27.
41. *Ibid.,* p. 25.
42. 'To Defend and Vindicate Our Rights', The Bruce Arnold on Monday column, *Irish Independent,* 13 July 1987.
43. *Ibid.* Author's italics.

Index

Abortion *see* Bunreacht na hEireann; Catholic Church
Acts of the Oireachtas:
   Censorship of Films (1923), 39; Censorship of Publications (1929), 39; Criminal
   Law Amendment (1935), 35, 53; European Communities (1972), 99, 100, 101, 102,
   109; Executive Authority (External Relations) (1936), 24; Extradition (1965), 123;
   Family Planning (Amendment), 53; Intoxicating Liquor (1927), 39; Public Dance
   Halls (1935), 39; Republic of Ireland (1948), 15, 24; Single European (1973), 18, 73,
   96, 99, 104, 106-116 *passim,* 120
Acts (British):
   Act of Union, 1800, 10; Ireland Act, 1949, 25; Offences against the Person Act,
   1861, 54
Alibrandi, Gaetano, 55
Amendments of the Constitution, 118 ff,
   Third, 96, 99, 101, 120; Fourth, 120; Fifth, 50, 120; Sixth, 120; Seventh, 120;
   Eighth, 55, 120; Ninth, 120; Tenth, 96, 99, 101, 112, 120
Anglo-Irish Agreement, 57, 92, 130
Arnold, Bruce, 130
Articles of Bunreacht na hEireann *see* Bunreacht na hEireann
Attlee, Clement, 15

Banting, Keith, 129
Barry, Peter, 110
Bowman, John, 22, 24-25, 26, 31, 82
Browne, Noel, 36, 40
Bunreacht na hEireann:
   Article 2, 16, 25, 29, 81-92 *passim,* 124, 127; Article 3, 16, 25, 29, 32, 81-92 *passim,*
   124, 127; Article 5, 23, 114, 115-16; Article 8, 20; Article 15, 27, 40, 60, 81; Article
   16, 3; Article 18, 27, 40; Article 19, 27, 40; Article 26, 61; Article 28, 61; Article 29,
   23-24, 97-98, 99, 100, 109, 112; Article 34, 60, 102-3; Article 40, 87, 120; Article 41,
   68, 84, 87, 124, 125; Article 42, 44, 68; Article 43, 68; Article 44, 21, 27-29, 31, 32,
   40, 41, 44, 49-52, 82, 84-85, 87, 120, 123; Article 45, 27, 61, 64, 66, 71; and abortion,
   54-55; and adoption, 120; and Catholic Church, 21, 26, 27-29, 33ff, 45ff; and
   constitutional law, 2, 3, 44, 62, 66ff; and the courts, 42-44, 60ff, 111, 117-18, 120;
   amendments of, 8, 32, 40, 50, 52ff, 83ff, 109-10, 113, 117, 119ff; and de Valera, 20ff,
   39, 40; and divorce, 55-59, 84, 127-28; and European Community law, 1, 8, 18, 96ff;
   and Irish language, 26, 29-30; and the natural law, 40, 42-44, 71-72; and Northern
   Ireland, 49, 79ff, 118-19, 123, 124-27; and referenda, 1, 56-57, 110, 118; and
   partition, 81, 91; and the United Kingdom, 9ff; amendments of, 8, 32, 40,50, 52ff,